Copyright © 2018 by Sandy C. Jayne

ISBN-13: 978-1717467898
ISBN-10: 171746789X

Cover illustration and layout by Cindy Anderson, Los Angeles, CA.
Character design by D. Allen, Eatontown, NJ.
Edited by Lisa Cohen, Belford, NJ.
Photos by John Ahrens, Keansburg, NJ.

Is This Seat Taken?

*A Diary of Random Thoughts,
Rants & Funny Sh*t
From a NYC Commuter*

Sandy C. Jayne

As the doors close and the train pulls away, I stare out the window and my mind starts to wander. Often to just random shit I've seen on social media or in the news, or even from some of the stupid conversations that go on around me while I sit and ponder.

Sometimes I get so caught up in my own thoughts that stuff goes on around me and I am clueless, until it hits me in the face, or sometimes in the back of the head.

So be prepared folks, while some of what you read might be crude, a lot of it is pretty funny.

Let us begin.....

Photo Credit: John Ahrens

Once Upon a Time…..
In the Beginning…..
In a Galaxy Far, Far Away…...
(You get the fucking point, just read!)

For over 21 years I have commuted into New York City to a job I had always dreamt about as a kid. Yes, that's right! The exciting, stressful world of corporate Wall Street! The life we all see and hear about on TV and in the movies. Yes, that was me, a young, still wet behind the ears 23-year-old chick from Jersey whose dream was to climb that corporate ladder and make a name for myself and gain the respect I desired and deserved. Over the years I have seen some really funny shit. Some of which was pretty fucked up shit!

You'll have to pardon my language as you read along, being from Jersey, I tend to drop a lot of F-bombs. I'm a lady who is often blunt and crass, so just stay with me on this ride and I promise, you will have a laugh, or two or 10.

My corporate life started when I began working in New York City in early-1995 and that was one bite of the Big Apple I wasn't quite prepared for. There were so many people all determined to get where they were going in the hustle and bustle of New York City life. And I craved all that madness. This is what I wanted - that "suit" life. I wanted power, I wanted respect and I wanted to be the boss. But mostly, I did it for the money. Yep! New York City was where I wanted to be to begin my career, whatever that was. I just knew that if I wanted to succeed in my professional growth, I needed to be there. I didn't go to college after high school, in fact, I couldn't wait to graduate high school, become independent and start making money. Boy was I a fool! Kids, if you're reading this...STAY IN SCHOOL FOR AS LONG AS YOU CAN! Or at least until your parents run out of money for your education! Seriously, trust me on this. Don't rush your life or you will end up looking back (like me) and wishing you could change things knowing what you know now.

I had to work twice as hard as the next person because I didn't have the education or the degree. But I worked my ass off and it took me as high as I could possibly go in my field as an event manager, and at the top of the salary range for my position.

During all of this, I began to write in my spare time in 1996, with no clue about what the fuck I was getting into. I just knew that I had a vivid, detailed imagination and that my words could actually make people visualize what I was writing about. I had a talent, but I also knew that this was a very competitive industry I was trying to break into. With as much enthusiasm as I could muster up at that time (and at a time where the internet was still in its infancy, and where Google, Amazon and Facebook didn't yet exist), I began to do some research into copyright and writing structure. I borrowed books from colleagues and asked a million questions from copyright lawyers I hardly knew which, to my surprise, were very encouraging and enthusiastic about answering my questions.

Possibilities on the horizon were endless and it seemed like an impossible dream, but it occupied my free time and I learned some interesting things along the way.

While doing my research, I decided that I needed to continue writing my manuscript because, much like now, my thoughts are always all over the place as my mind tends to work faster than I can type. I didn't want to forget a single detail about the story I was compiling in my head and I began to work on a fictional, suspense novel. I was damn proud of how far I had come with the manuscript but at the same time, my career started to take off and I had to put aside my writing project…..sigh…..

Over the years I've started and stopped this project many times. During my downtime at work, I would often open up the manuscript and pick up where I left off. But, as fate would have it, work got busy…..again. It finally got so busy at work that I put the writing project aside altogether and over time and with life, it was forgotten.

In 2015 my step-father, having been diagnosed with several forms of cancer, had become gravely ill. I lost my mother in 2006 to breast cancer and it never gets any easier seeing a loved one suffer from this dreadful disease. I took a few days off from work to be with my family during his last days. Sadly, within a few short days, he passed.

About a week later, after helping my family with funeral arrangements and settling my step-father's estate, I returned to work where I learned that within several months, I would be losing my job due to a department restructuring. On July 1, 2016, after 21 years with the firm that I considered my second home, I was let go. Ironically, this same day was the 10 year anniversary of my mother's death. I was crushed and extremely emotional that day. I hadn't the foggiest idea of where I was going to go, nor what I was going to do next. I was lost. It felt like everything bad was happening all at once and anxiety and depression began to consume me. I came to a realization that I was starting all over again, only this time I was in my 40's with a home and a family and I was terrified.

In between rebuilding my resume, filing for unemployment, searching for a job, writing cover letter after boring cover letter, scheduling phone calls and interviews, working a part-time job cleaning houses and a part-time job in retail, I'd often dive into writing short excerpts, a diary of sorts, based on my experiences and observations during my commutes to and from New York City.

Some of which were just rants of what irritated me at that moment or simply based on reflections of all my experiences over the years. Whatever I was feeling at that moment, my fingers feverishly typed! Sometimes these moments made me sad, sometimes they made me laugh but they all had the same end result….it took away the anxiety I was feeling, even if it was just for a little while. My imagination got carried away with me and I cracked myself up. I wanted to share these excerpts. To gauge how people would react to my writing, I would sometimes post my thoughts on social media which, to my surprise, received a great reaction from friends and family. It's at that moment that I knew I had to get back to writing, and quickly!

Let me tell you this…..writer's block? It is VERY real! The more stress you have in your life, the less focus and motivation you have to do the things you love. I was afraid of losing concentration on my writing project, again. I needed a brief distraction so I turned to social media for a few laughs. I reconnected with an acquaintance, D. Allen, whom I'd met through an old friend and co-worker in the mid-90's. We exchanged messages and I learned that he was a writer. At that time, he invited me to like a page that he managed where

he'd written and shared his thoughts from a man's perspective on life, love, relationships, marriage, kids, friendships, sex and any other topic that struck him in the moment. I really liked his writing style. He mentioned to me that he had written some short stories in the past which were "much different" than the style of what he wrote on his page. Being a very curious person, I asked to see a sample. Cautious and hesitant at first, he finally sent it to me.........
Well, I'd be lying if I didn't say that the story wasn't anything short of steamy!

HOLY SHIT!!

As I read through it, my mind was spinning off ideas and I saw an opportunity before me. I sent back a message to him, a couple of long days later, asking if I could add to it and edit. To his anticipated relief, he replied "sure!!" I added my perspective as a woman, softened some things here and there and added a bit more description so that the story had more build-up...and, of course...release (hee, hee!) We talked about writing together and I discussed the idea that I had with him, we expanded on that idea and embarked on a new writing project. We wrote in a "ping-pong" fashion in the erotica genre which offered the perspectives of a man and a woman.

Our book, *Bedtime Stories: His Words, Her Desires* was published in October 2017. It was one of the most exciting times in my life, I was finally pursuing my dream to become an author. We fucking did it! Our book was out there! I was so high that I thought it would be impossible to come back down. Sadly, within a few months, despite our best efforts to market it, we were just little fish in a very big pond. Sales began to fizzle out as we started to blend into the background with other books of the same genre.

I was completely crushed because I had high expectations. But, that was not going to get me down. In fact, I was determined to push further by exploring other possibilities and changing genres, again. Which brings me to the present day!

During the marketing of *Bedtime Stories*, I've met some amazing people along the way. I've had some pretty insightful conversations with a few of them (you know who you are! 😁) but all of them had similar advice for me. Keep writing!

Being a writer and working three jobs has its challenges. Since I have no one to hold me accountable, I was forced to do a lot of networking and promoting myself as a writer. I am always grateful to those who have offered to help me and although I don't have a lot of spare time, I try to squeeze in a post once or twice a week on social media, just to keep myself visible, which often takes my time away from doing the writing for my book.

I have some great friends and family who have been so supportive and I am truly blessed for both their friendship and their belief in me to stand beside me and lift me up as I pursue this dream. (By the way, if you haven't read *Bedtime Stories: His Words, Her Desires*, pick up a copy on Amazon today. If you like erotic romance and fantasies of real men and women, then you will not be disappointed! It'll put the spice, in your spicy meatball!)

Not everything you will read here happened in New York City but rather during my commutes to and from the City, or from things I've witnessed or overheard. A lot of my thoughts were provoked and writings initiated while riding the bus, train or subway, and occasionally on the ferry, or while I drove to work (yes, I did drive several times into New York City, and those stories alone can fill another book!). My OCD wants to keep these things in date order however, some of these just don't seem funny unless you read an earlier entry first. So bear with me, and I promise to make this fun for you!

As you read along, please keep an open mind. I'd like you to see these events though my eyes. While my compilations are based on many years of witnessing some of the most off-the-wall shit (and I mean the kind of shit you just can't make up!) I spent a lot of time watching people and observing their quirky behavior. Sometimes I walked right into it and the timing couldn't be more perfect, and other times I just needed to run like hell from it!

While there are many adventures over the years as a commuter, I've included for you some highlights that I hope will make you laugh. So sit back, grab a glass of wine or a beer, relax and enjoy this ride!

Photo Credit: John Ahrens

Eww, That's Gross!

You know what I find hilarious? The stuff that most normal people would not. The kind of stuff we're "not supposed to talk about" in public. You know, potty humor! Farting, burping, sharing shit and puke stories - the all-around grossities that most do not laugh at, or the stuff we're supposed to keep in the bedroom, or the bathroom. Potty humor is what keeps us "real" as people. But the stuff we're "not supposed to talk about" creates some of the funniest stories to tell! Comedians would have a really hard time doing stand-up if they couldn't tell dick, fart and shit jokes. Come on, everybody poops! They even wrote a book about it! And if we can't discuss our (sometimes funny) antics in the bedroom? Well, then you might as well slap a chastity belt on me and call me a virgin! What can I say, I'm a hot mess chick with a dirty mind who still laughs at fart jokes!

Diary Entry - June 28, 2018

So today started off with a bang! Woke up to a thunderstorm and pouring rain this morning (which is cool when you don't have to get ready for work). Started getting ready as the lights flickered and I prayed that the power would not go out while I was in the middle of putting on my face and doing my hair. But, what the hell was the purpose of doing my hair anyway? It's all soupy and swamp-assy outside - so up in a clip it goes! Got dressed in a brand new t-shirt I bought last year that apparently just hung in my closet all year. Pulled a Bruce Springsteen and checked my look in the mirror. I stuck my tongue out at my own reflection as I was completely unsatisfied with the way I looked and now I *"wanna change my clothes, my hair, my face"*!! (I know you sang that!) I closed the closet door as my daughter looks me over like a mom with a disapproving look.

"You're going to work in that shirt?" She said, with a hint of sarcasm in her voice.

"Yes, why?" I replied, with concern.

"Well it's covered in lint balls!"

I look down and say, "No it's not, it's the pattern of the shirt."

"Well, it looks like you dried it in the dryer with a bunch of white towels" she said, as she bit into her granola bar and walked away.

I shake my head and now I keep thinking maybe she was right! Time check....6:40, fuck! No time to change. I put on my cute, strappy, wedge sandals that I got on clearance at Kohl's last year for $7.00 - totes adorbs! My daughter, once again, looks me over.

"Are you sure you wanna wear those?"

"Ugh, jeez kid, why now?" I said, rather annoyed.

"Umm, because it's pouring outside and your feet are gonna get wet!"

I ignore the kid, just grab my purse and walked out. I caught a break in the downpour in just enough time to sprint to my car. I pull out of the driveway and a monsoon hits! My wipers aren't working fast enough as I'm driving just 25 MPH! Coffee? Fuck Quick Check, there's no time! I get on the parkway, and I know I've bitched about this shit before, but the frikken material they use in the asphalt that they paved the road in just sucks big donkey ass! I can't see shit in front of me as the back kick from the tires of the cars in front of me made it seem like I was driving through fog! For fucks sake, we pay enough in god damn taxes and tolls in this state! Quit being a bunch of penny-pinching prickfaces and pave the damn road with better shit! I remember years ago the roads were much better to drive on in bad weather.

Anyway, I made it to work in a decent amount of time, considering the weather. I stopped at 7-11 for my coffee - which is complete crap and I paid 50 cents more for the same size cup than I do at Quick Check! So I paid $2.12 for a cup of crap! I get to work and it starts pouring again as I'm getting out of the car. I quickly run to the door, swipe my pass key and step inside. Took two steps on the tile floor, slip and down I went. I yell "motherfucker" really loud as I'm falling which felt like a slow-motion movie scene. Umm....did I mention that I work in a Catholic school? Yeah, I'm going to Hell! The good news is that I managed to keep my coffee upright with minimal spillage. No damage, no broken bones or bruises, no rips in the ass of my jeans - OK we're good!

I go to my office and get settled in. I'm checking my messages on the office line and writing shit down. I set the phone on my shoulder and grabbed my coffee and took a big sip through the straw (shut up, I sip my coffee through a straw - bite me!) and swallow. I cringed as I just realized my coffee is cold and that I had taken a huge sip and swallowed the coffee from yesterday's cup (which I mistakenly left on my desk, next to the phone). It didn't taste sour so what's the worst that could happen, right? I move the cup to the other side of my desk and grabbed my fresh cup. I'd empty the old cup later when I had some time.

An hour passed and I'm headed to the bathroom to empty my cup. I open it up and look down. There's two giant dead carpenter ants floating in it. And I sipped that shit! Gross!

But.....I'm wearing cute sandals and a cool color polish on my toes, so there's that!

Diary Entry - May 4, 2018

This morning as I got into my car, I realized that it was covered in a pretty thick layer of yellow dust. It had me thinking.......Isn't pollen just like massive amounts of tree or flower sperm, dusting everything? Yeah, think about THAT the next time you take a slow, deep breath in while you're outside on this warm, Spring day! Take it all in deep, baby. You're welcome!

Diary Entry - July 23, 2015

On the train tonight and sitting in a somewhat empty car of the train, probably because the AC isn't working so great. I find a seat to myself and get comfortable, scrolling through Facebook. I look up because I hear this strange noise in front of me, a pig-like honk. I look in the reflection of the window next to where I hear this strange noise only to find that some dude was blowing air hankies! Then, he starts picking his nose, I mean he was mining for those boogers! I think his finger got lost at the bridge of his nose on the way to his eyeball!

Diary Entry - May 8, 2014

A guy gets on the train in Newark. It's a double-decker train, half empty and he decides to sit in the window seat, which is directly across the aisle from me. He starts chatting me up with small talk then moves to the seat closer to the aisle to continue our conversation. The guy has a moving bat in the cave and what appears to be spinach caught between his teeth. He reeks of alcohol, garlic and ass breath. (For those who do not know what a "bat in the cave" is, it is a visible, dangling booger that the person may not be aware of unless they looked in a mirror. NOTE: Always be sure to check those tunnels after blowing to be sure you've cleared all obstructions!) Just when I thought it couldn't get any worse, the guy starts laughing hysterically and the bat comes flying out of the cave and sticks to the back of the seat in front of him. It was totally gross, but funny at the same time. It took everything I had to contain my laughter!

Diary Entry - September 12, 2014

I'm sitting on the subway and I hear this guy laughing in the seat across the aisle from me. So of course I *had* to look. A wacky, older man was laughing hysterically at something on his phone and I noticed he had the biggest booger I've ever seen dangling from his right nostril (another bat in the cave). I could be wrong, but I think that thing waved to me! Why do I always seem to zone in on these things?

Diary Entry - September 10, 2014

To add to my hatred and germ phobia of the train, this morning I watched some guy stick his hand down the back of his pants to scratch his ass, then grabbed the railing with the same hand as he held and read the newspaper with the other! Eww! I will continue to either wait for a seat or "subway surf" but I sure as hell ain't touching those railings!

Diary Entry - April 9, 2014

It's funny the things that some people will do when they think no one is watching......or they just don't care.....kudos to you buddy! Get that finger way up there and scratch the back of your eyeball while you're at it!

Diary Entry - December 3, 2013

The doors open on the subway car and the people file in, quickly scrambling to find an empty seat. I happened to luck out and grab the first end seat next to the doors. As the train became more crowded, a guy is standing next to me, leaning against the railing of the seat, he's standing to the left of me. My long hair is slightly hanging over the railing and every so often I felt a tug as he moved against the railing. Without warning, he decided to shove his hand down the back of his pants to scratch his ass and pulled my hair along with it - ugh! Must people stand that fucking close when doing nasty shit like that? I wanna puke - and I need a shower! Gross....

Diary Entry - October 9, 2013

I hate commuting during non-rush hour times. Bunch of ass clowns on the train. Drunk guy decides he can't wait for the bathroom so he pees in a beer bottle. And you can guess what happens next? Yep, bottle falls over and pee runs down the train under the seat ......ugh! What a douchebag! Spent the rest of my night with my feet on the seat. Just let one of those douchebag conductors tell me to put my feet down and I will kick him in the gullet!

Diary Entry - January 18, 2013

Dear people on the train: Do you find it necessary to suck up all that snot and clear your throat obnoxiously while standing right over me?? REALLY?? Didn't your mama teach you better

than that? That's disgusting! Have a little class and
respect for others around you. I understand people
have allergies or colds but still, do it AWAY from
people or next time my half-digested breakfast will
be all over your shoes!

Speaking of snot-sucking……

Diary Entry - February 11, 2008

While commuting this morning, I sat next to
one of the regulars who rides the bus at the same
time I do each morning. Sometimes we chat, and
sometimes I'm too tired to utter a word that I just
drift off to sleep. This one morning I couldn't sleep
because the person behind me kept coughing and
blowing their nose. It's kind of hard to sleep with
all that snot-sucking going on behind me (which by
the way is extremely nauseating!). So I strike up a
conversation with the woman sitting next to me and
at that moment, the person behind me sneezed in the
most disgusting manner that I actually felt the
breeze come around and over the seat. The woman
next to me and I look at each other with disgust but
then didn't think anything else of it as we continued
our conversation.

A few hours later I am now at work, having a meeting with my staff about events coming up. I turned my head to pick up something from the desk behind me and my one staff member says to me,

"What's in your hair? Did a bird shit on you?"

Perplexed, I said, "What do you mean?" as I touched the back of my head.

"Wait, let me help you," she said, as she tried to untangle my hair.

"Eww, it's all dried and hard. Let's go into the ladies room and I'll help you get it out."

We go into the ladies room and I looked in the giant mirror and turned to try and see the back of my head. I gagged and nearly tossed my cookies as I realized that what I was looking at was a giant glob of dried phlegm! That disgusting piece of shit on the bus didn't even have the decency to admit to sneezing it on my head!

Why are people so gross? Seriously, if you're sick, stay the fuck home! Or at the very least, cover your mouth when you cough or sneeze, fucker!

Photo Credit: John Ahrens

What's That Smell?

I think you can guess where this is headed. Yes, we are human and sometimes, well…..we stink! Literally! Crowded subway cars and buses, often with no air conditioning on some of the hottest days of the year, can lead to some sticky and stinky situations, and cranky passengers (myself included)! And even when it is not hot and sticky, there is always some asshole on the train who thinks it's funny to let one rip on a crowded train.

For many of us with a relatively good hygiene regime, we often don't realize that we stink, for whatever reason. We could shower three times but nothing will help the rancid garlic that comes out of our pores. The best we can hope for is some breath mints, perfume or cologne and even some lotion. I don't know about you folks out there, but I have a pretty sensitive nose and my sense of smell is heightened. And for all the funk that resides on the train, there is no escape and there is no window to open to air out the putrid stench. Instead we are forced to marinate in it until we can no longer smell it - or until the tiny hairs in our noses are so singed that we have lost all sense of smell.

Diary Entry - January 6, 2016

It's a new year and my first commuting story for 2016! Today was my first day back to work since December 29. I'm on the train this morning sitting on the end seat where I normally sit (predictable I know, but what can I say, I am a creature of habit!) It's only a 22-minute train ride from Newark to WTC so I shut my eyes, but was not exactly asleep. There's a man standing up right next to me, leaning against the door. The train pulls into Grove Street and just before the doors open, he lets one rip! 💨💨💨 I quickly turn my head in a very *I heard that* stare. As I turned my head, the breeze from the open doors blows his ass gas right in my face! It was just as bad as a Dutch oven - no lie! His ass was that close to my head that I could practically taste what he ate for dinner the night before! I couldn't contain myself or the expression of agony on my face and quickly shook my head like a cartoon character in a feeble attempt to whip the stench away from my nostrils. Nice job, fucker!

Diary Entry - November 24, 2015

So I'm on the train, kind of hunched down low in the seat, which is the norm for me after a long day. When out of nowhere the dude behind me not only burps disgustingly, but proceeds to blow it all over the place which smelled like a rancid #3 sub! I wait about five seconds, then I slowly peek over the top of my seat. There he is looking right at me with a look of shock and embarrassment on his face. I guess he was surprised to find that someone was sitting in the seat in front of him. The look on his face was priceless as I sat back down in my seat and chuckled to myself. I still find this shit funny. I'm such a child!

Diary Entry - September 23, 2015

Shocker! Another commuting story for you bitches! I'm sitting on the train last night and we just pulled out of World Trade Center. There was a guy standing next to me about two people over (his voice was really deep, and kind of loud, and I couldn't help but listen to him). He was talking to a pregnant woman standing next to him who looked like she was ready to puke. Out of nowhere he says to another guy standing behind the pregnant woman with his arm over her shoulder to hold the bar (for purposes of this story, I will refer to them as Guy 1 and Stinky Guy).

Guy 1: "Man, you stink, don't you use deodorant? Phew!"

Stinky Guy: (totally stone-faced and serious) "I haven't used deodorant in a long time. I don't use soap either"

At this point people were backing away from him. He was ripe!

Guy 1: "Man, how can you stand yourself?"

Stinky Guy: "I don't stink"

I almost burst out laughing, looking at the faces of other people standing around him holding their nose and rolling their eyes. This guy also had on those short, satin running shorts and I can only imagine that if he doesn't use soap, what that "area" must smell like. Can you imagine some woman going down on him and is slapped in the face by his soupy, ball sweat smell, combined with onion soup? OMG I think I just threw up in my mouth a little! Anyway….

.

Guy 1: "Man, you don't smell that? You need deodorant."

Stinky Guy: (again, stone-faced and serious) "No, deodorant is bad."

Guy 1: "Uhhh, NO….no it's not, it's GOOD and keeps you from stinking up the place, unless you like your armpits to smell like a dirty ass!"

Hahahahahaha! At this point I could no longer contain my laughter. After the Grove Street stop, a bunch of people got off and who do you think this guy stood right in front of until the next stop with his swampy, stinky pits and his crotch in my face? ME!! Why am I a fucking magnet for all that shit? Gross!

Diary Entry - April 13, 2015

I'm on a super crowded train this evening with delays because of police activity and the air conditioning isn't quite right on this rather warm April day, and some people haven't adjusted their deodorant levels yet. Some guy barrels me over to grab a seat, no apology for his behavior, such a rude douchebag! So now I'm standing in a dress and heels with some guy's stinky, salami-smelling armpit in my face. I was gagging and nearly puking when saw him use his free hand to pick his nose while he looked at me! Eww! I turned my back to him at the next stop since a little room freed up only to find another guy standing to my left picking *his* nose too! Do you people not have any manners or self-respect to mine for your boogers in private? Totally skeeved out right now. I'll need to shower TWICE tonight!

Diary Entry - June 11, 2014

A guy was standing in front of me on the train as we pull into Newark. He doesn't realize that I'm standing literally right behind him waiting to get off. Just before the doors open, this guy lets out a deep belch and yep, I walk right through it! I couldn't hide my gasping expression as he turned around to apologize when he realized someone was standing behind him! How do you respond to that? "Oh, it's OK, no problem!" No, it's NOT OK, you just burped practically in my face with your garlic, rancid assbreath!

Diary Entry - April 29, 2014

I'm sitting next to a guy on the train this morning who has horrible breath and smells like a combination of wet dog and swamp ass. And as he reads, he keeps sighing, blowing his stink all over the place! What a lovely way to start my day! <blech>

Diary Entry - February 26, 2014

Maybe it's just that I have a very sensitive sense of smell, or some people really do hang their clothes in the kitchen while cooking. There is a guy in the row in front of me and the smell that is emanating from him is so fucking gross! How do you tell someone that they reek? My nose is buried in my scarf and I still smell him - yuck!

Diary Entry - July 26, 2012

P-U!! The guy sitting next to me on the train smells like he went dumpster diving! Yuck!

Diary Entry - April 27, 2012

I'm a freak magnet for smelly people, nose pickers and spit-talkers! (Hmmm, sounds like most people on the train) I swear I'm gonna hurl!

Diary Entry - July 9, 2012

People, you REALLY need to partake in the wearing of deodorant in this hot weather. Granted, it's not 100 degrees today however, in a crowded train it can get unwelcomely cozy and I don't need to be subjected to your rotten, salami-smelling nastiness. Thank you and have a good day! (P.S. is "unwelcomely" even a real word??)

Diary Entry - July 19, 2012

Dear Summertime Commuters: Deodorant. It's really nice.......it's your BFF! For the love of Pete and for the sake of your fellow commuters, use it people! Either I just have a keen sense of smell, or some people are just stinky bitches!

Diary Entry – April 22, 2010

I'm on the bus going home and we're stuck in traffic at a standstill. I'm sitting next to a woman who fell asleep with her mouth open. I should toss in some tiny mints and take pictures! OMG, the stink!!

Photo Credit: John Ahrens

Phone Shit

Nowadays everyone is on their smartphones while commuting. It's almost impossible to commute without one, myself included! Whether you use it to browse social media, read the news, shop or listen to music, it seems that the smartphone, or a tablet of some sort, has replaced the laptop while commuting.

I'm addicted to the games on my phone because it helps to pass the time. Between the various notification sounds, ringtones and media sounds it's a wonder anyone can get in any decompression time before going home to the chaos of family life with children and animals. I like to relax most of the way home. It's my time to just observe, think and, well, write all this shit down for you!

Diary Entry - March 29, 2018

Why do I always seem to get caught goofing off by my male co-worker? First time I was spitting out a bad nut (a pistachio, you naughty perverts), this time I was looking through silly, yet perverted gifs which I was going to send to my like-minded girlfriends in a group text (y'all know who you are!) and I thought I had closed my screen when he walked in. I set the phone down and looked up at him, not realizing my phone's screen was still open. I see him looking down at my desk so naturally I looked down too. Yep, goofy, animated erections were just playing for him to see as my face turned beet red and an instant hot flash came over me. Dancing cartoon dicks everywhere!! OMG, now he thinks I'm a pervert! Wait, well yes that would be a correct assumption! He just laughed and shook his head as his face turned red too. But, it's a silly, perverted sense of humor I have. All in good fun but embarrassed is an understatement!

Diary Entry - July 7, 2015

I hate when people are so engulfed in their phones when they are walking that they do not pay attention to what's around them. Twice today I've had people plow right into me because they were looking down at their phones. I'm going to start carrying a hockey stick so I can crosscheck those idiots! How's that for a visual on a crowded city street at rush hour? Ha!

Diary Entry - October 27, 2014

Some people think they are so slick when they think they are alone on the train. Tonight I'm sitting in a seat alone and there is a guy in front of me. We are both sitting against the window. It is now dusk and the reflection in the windows on the train act like a mirror. So, I'm nosey and I see that he has his phone turned toward the window which gave me a clear view of what he was looking at. Porn! Yep, he was watching dirty movies on his phone! Sinner.....

Diary Entry - September 27, 2012

The girl next to me on the train tonight has her headphones on and she is rapping rather badly and very loudly, "All I want for ma birfday is a big booty ho!" Really? I mean they make headphones for a reason, ya know! Lip sync or something, just shut the fuck up already, I'm trying to sleep!

Diary Entry - August 10, 2012

So this morning while on a very quiet train, I am playing a game on my phone and my friend sends me a text message. Having forgot to turn down the volume on my phone, the text message comes across with a very loud "*BAZZINGA*!" It was quite comical to look up and see that all eyes were on me. I was beet red in the face, as I see people chuckling - but I had the courage to muster up a squeaky "sorry!"

Diary Entry - August 17, 2012

So the infamous text notification on my phone strikes again!! This time I just stepped in a crowded elevator at my office when my dear friend sends me a text message. Mind you, I just recently changed my text notification from "*Bazzinga*" to something a lot less acceptable in today's professional world. In any event, I feel the buzz in my bag before I hear the audio and I pray to myself "oh god no, please don't be loud!" But alas, a very loud "*MAIL MOTHERFUCKER*" not once, but THREE MOTHERFUCKING TIMES! You'd think I would have learned my lesson from last week's incident on the train. I'm completely mortified! Thanks a lot my friend!

Diary Entry - July 13, 2012

I'm developing a new app for my phone, similar to Angry Birds. I'm going to call it Angry People. This game will allow you to upload a face pic of the person or persons getting on your nerves in place of the little Angry Birds. Then you can launch them into a brick wall and watch them "pop" as they disappear!

Ahhh, I can already feel the stress leaving my body!

Photo Credit: John Ahrens

Totally Random Thoughts
& Funny Rants
*(That may or may not have anything
to do with commuting!)*

I have about an hour and 30-minute commute home which gives me a lot of time to just sit and think. I look around, browse social media, or pretend to sleep while I eavesdrop on some juicy conversations. Sometimes I go into too much detail and I wish people were in my head to understand the way I think. I can take something totally random and make up a story around it, just by observation alone. I sometimes crack myself up and can't help but laugh out loud at the visuals that I compile in my head. There is seriously something wrong with me!

Diary Entry – December 7, 2018

OK folks - time for another one of my rants! As I drove home this evening, stuck in a bit of traffic and steaming over what I just heard on the radio, prompted me to write this little gem.

Why are there so many snowflakes out there? I'm so tired of people being offended by every goddamned thing every time you turn around! A song, a color, a flag, fucking candy canes, TV shows, books, pictures, even people (celebrities, politicians, comedians). Come on people, just grow the fuck up already! For most of you, all of the things you are "offended" by have been in existence since before you were born! It's a part of our history and clearly shows how far we have come as a society.

"Baby It's Cold Outside" - are you fucking kidding me with this?? Yet, screaming obscenities in rock, country, pop or rap songs or other sex and drinking and drug-related songs don't offend you? Where are your priorities? "Baby It's Cold Outside" is a classic, holiday song, and it's only played around the holidays for fuck's sake - only 30 or so days! Get over yourselves you little assholes!

The way things offend you, you might as well paint everyone gray, take away their manparts and ladyparts, dress them in a single uniform and let them walk around without belief in anything, take away their hopes and dreams and don't let them have any fun. A life filled with nothing but zombies. Doesn't sound like a life I'd want to live!

Pretty soon fairytale movies will offend you little douchenuggets. Cinderella - clearly a movie about mental abuse and bullying, but with a happy ending. Why doesn't this offend you? Yet the Rudolph the Red-Nosed Reindeer offends you. Because you're a snowflake and you're living in the "moment" and jumping on the bandwagon. Maybe you just don't like that song or other songs like it. So fucking what??!! There are a lot of songs I don't like but you don't see me taking it to the media! Frosty the Snowman – don't get me started. He was a jolly, happy soul and you want to melt him out of existence?

Carol - as in Christmas Carol - why does it have to be a woman's name? Oh wait, does that offend you too? Maybe it should be called a Christmas John and we can be Johnning all over the place.......would that make you feel better??

(Johnning? Why do I have this vision in my head of people peeing everywhere? - Man, I'm so dumb sometimes! Ha ha!)

Hey, you know what? I'm offended by YOU, ya little snowflakes, how's that suit ya? Quit harshin' my mellow with your bullshit. You're really acting like douchebags!

I'll suck on my candy canes, watch Rudolph and sing along to as many "offensive" Christmas "Carols" as I please - and at the top of my lungs! Oh wait, does singing offend you? Are you offended by snowflakes too? Or does just the term offend you?

I'll say Merry Christmas to my Christian friends, Happy Channukah to my Jewish friends and Happy Festivus to the rest of us! I'm not going to change my beliefs or sacrifice my happiness because I'm afraid to offend others with my celebration of the holiday season.

Oh, and if this post offends any of my friends - just scroll on by and feel free to delete me if you wish. Your negative comments are not welcome on my wall! Opinions are like assholes, everybody's got one - and I'm a big one! Wait..... what?

In all seriousness - relax a bit folks – it's the holidays! Time for spreading joy and cheer, not anger and hate! I'd be nothing without a sense of humor in a world we all take too seriously at times.

Diary Entry – September 21, 2018

My boobs could open a delicatessen with the amount of food I harvest from them. I'd call it "*Sandy's Boobicatessen.*" Today's lunch special includes bits of ham and shredded lettuce, with a side of chip! Yes, during my lunch today, I looked down and found a piece of ham, a string of shredded lettuce and a piece of a potato chip wedged in my cleavage. Thank god the mayo didn't find its way there or I might have had some explaining to do!

Diary Entry – June 20, 2018

Seems like every third post I scroll past has some sort of political rant or opinion of some little asshole sitting behind a keyboard saying *"Imma bout to stir some shit - mwahahaha!"* I don't care what side you're on, but please, for the love of Pete, for one day could you please, please, PLEASE post pics of your kids or dogs or food or your gym workouts? Hell, I think a picture of your giant, stinky crap in a toilet bowl would be more interesting and a refreshing relief to the other shit you're posting! When did social media become such a dick to scroll through? And don't even get me started on Twitter, she's a twat! If Twitter and Facebook had a political baby, they'd name it Twittface because, well...do I really need to explain this one??

Diary Entry - May 17, 2018

Here's a newsflash! I don't give a flying, hairy vagina about Laurel and Yanni, I hear both, OK? Because I'm just *that* fucking awesome with my supersonic hearing! Seriously?? This is what's clogging my social media newsfeed? This is like that fucking white/gold or black/blue dress debacle of 2015! Who gives a shit?? Here, I'll just give you the shit, wrapped in a white/gold bow (or is it black/blue?).....Whatever, just go away with that nonsense shit! What a bunch of asswipes!

Diary Entry - May 6, 2018

Mochacino, latte, cappucino, macchiato, espresso, frappe, frappacino.....what the hell happened to just plain coffee??? I'm tired of this fancy-schmancy, "pinky out", tiny cup, pretentious bullshit you identify as coffee. You've pussified MY coffee. Just gimme a large cup of Joe with cream and sugar and I'll be just fine, thank you! Fuck your fancy shittacino! And don't even get me started on the pumpkin spice shit!

Diary Entry - March 23, 2018

As April is almost upon us, today as I was scrolling through social media while I wait for my doctor appointment, I saw a t-shirt that said "*I don't cuss like a Sailor, I cuss like an April Lady.*" I thought about this for a minute. Now you people reading this and all of my other rants and random thoughts throughout this book, know that this could not be true about me. Nah, fuck that! I cuss like a two-dollar hooker with dirty knees! I make truck drivers blush!

Diary Entry - March 19, 2018

For a long time now I've been wearing glasses. The glasses I have now are the perfect shape/style for my face. I got contacts recently so I can wear them on occasion, however, because I can't see without my glasses, I never realized the dark circles under my eyes until I put my contacts in and I look in the mirror and think, *"Holy shit, who the fuck punched me in the peepers?"* Then I wonder, *"Shit, you ugly bitch, have you always looked like this without glasses?"* Maybe I should drink a little more, put on my beer goggles and try again. OK, there we go *(as I look in the mirror).....*

"Damn baby, you're fine as hell! Wanna go make out?"

Diary Entry - February 8, 2018

It seems nowadays we are all attached to some sort of electronic device (phone, tablet, etc.) One of the things I have noticed lately is that a lot of the younger generation tend to speak and act as though they are part of those electronics. For example...conversation at work went something like this:

Girl 1: *"OMG, I totes forgot to call my Dad, he's gonna kill me!"*

Girl 2: *"OMG, I legit LOL'd at the look on your face when you said that!"*

All I could do was shake my head and giggle. I mean, when the fuck did texting acronyms become part of our daily speech?? A couple of days later I am looking through pictures with a friend and I found myself "pinching" the picture to enlarge it, not realizing that it was an actual picture and NOT on my phone! SMH......

Diary Entry - February 2, 2018

Groundhog Day - dumbest day ever! And why do we waste our time, media and tax dollars on all this shit? I mean come on! A rodent doesn't predict anything folks! Shadow? What shadow? Does he even know what a shadow is? Get a grip people! He only came out of his hole looking around for some food and took one look at your ugly faces staring at him and said, *"Aaahhh! Fuck this, I'm cold, you people are assholes, I'm going back in my hole! I'll be back to tear up your lawn when it's warm out! Hasta la vista, bitches!"*

That guy..... is a friggen jerk....

Diary Entry - January 29, 2018

I hate cinnamon flavored anything. No gum, candy or cinnamon flavored alcohol. I'm always excited to eat the red jelly beans thinking that they are cherry or fruit punch flavored or those red and white candies that look exactly like peppermint until I get tongue-punched by cinnamon! This ruins my day. Fucking cinnamon, you need to rot in the fiery depths of Hell, where you came from!

Diary Entry - December 15, 2017

Last night, on my way home from a Christmas party in the City, I'm waiting in a line of cars three lanes wide, as we slowly merge into the Holland Tunnel. Three lanes are merging into one and I'm in the middle lane. This douchenozzle in a Tahoe on my left throws a full cup of coffee out his passenger window and hits my window with a thud that scared the fucking brownies out of me! With his window still open, he screams at me "let me in, you fucking cunt!" I was shocked and a little shook up that this fucker was so violent with his actions and his words, and nearly hitting my car as he forced his way in front of me.

My response? High beams the whole way through the tunnel! Merry Christmas, dickhead! I hope you choke on an eggplant!

Diary Entry – July 16, 2017

Stamp on eyebrows, magnetic eyelashes, strapless & backless suction cup cleavage enhancer, booty-lifting bodyshapers, lipstick that doesn't rub off.....all these things are hiding true beauty. WTF? It's becoming easier and easier to look as fake as a Barbie doll these days.

Diary Entry - June 6, 2017

So here's a rant, I'm sure my lady friends will understand this..... faux banded tops.

These tops were not made for women with big boobs. There is no way that anyone over a small C-cup could rock that shit. Trust me, I've tried. Now, while the style is super flattering on most women, us big titty chicks always get the short end of the stick. Gathered material looks great but it's just not wide enough from top to bottom. Fitted tops in general, which look great on a lot of women, just look ridiculous on me. I mean, how the fuck did Dolly

Parton make that shit look good? Oh, right, she had it custom made or tailored for her frame. I can't afford that shit, but dammit, I wanna look cute and sexy too! I'm not a size triple E or anything like that but I swear, unless you're a C-cup, it's just not going to look right unless you're wearing spandex or some other shit that hugs your body - and with that material, you have *other* problems to worry about!

I've also tried those fitted, button-down tops that have some "give" in them and I tried on a size that I would normally wear, but that fucking shit said "No way, bitch! You need a bigger size to get them puppies inside!" Yet here I am squeezing, digging and shifting my borderline DD's into this button-down top because on any normal day, THIS IS MY FUCKING SIZE! I look myself over in the mirror and noticed that the seams between the buttons are gaping and ready to burst like an overgrown zit on the face of a hormonal teen! So what do I do? I roll my shoulders forward in an uncomfortable manner to ease the tension on the seams to see how the shirt would look on me if I had smaller boobs. Now I look just fucking ridiculous so I throw my shoulders back and watch the buttons pop open as my boobs bounce free and relax (yeah guys, I saw the hot blonde visual too as she shook her head and hair playfully and smiled sexily......*sigh*........)

Anyway, I'm now frustrated and I get the next largest size as I curse under my breath, angry that I have to try this fucking thing on AGAIN! And I'm starting to second guess if it's even worth the extra trip back to the dressing room, yet I do it. I put the shirt on, again. Now while it fits in the breastal area, the shoulders are too big, sleeves are too long and I have all this extra material hanging from my tit area down the front, like I was wearing a maternity shirt, ugh! Pissed off, I take the fucking thing off, put it on the hanger inside out and unbuttoned because I'm so mad all I want to do is set the fucking shirt on fire and leave! And don't get me started on bras - why do bras for big-titty bitches like me look like you just purchased one of those backpack/sling thingies for twin babies! WTF???

Ahh, the frustrations we have as women shoppers. It's no wonder men look like they want to kill themselves when they go shopping with us!

Diary Entry - March 27, 2017

Bodyshapers.....Ladies, I have been seeing these waist cinchers and bodyshaper advertisements and videos all over my social media newsfeed and trust me when I tell you, they DON'T work!

First, if you got a little "extra lovin", where do you think all that shit goes when you put one of those things on? It has to go somewhere, right? Now, I'm not the thinnest of girls and I do have my curves and while I agree that it's good for smoothing out the lumps and bumps and all the imperfections, it forces your "extra lovin'" to other parts (i.e. your butt, legs, upper back) or accentuates them to look larger than if you *didn't* wear it.

Second, if you are wearing an already form fitting garment before putting it on, keep in mind that it adds an extra layer to your clothes, making you look like your clothes are even tighter.

Third, and most importantly, while we all strive to look our best, those fucking things are so uncomfortable and you spend half the night adjusting it and smoothing out the creases and indentations (because, of course, it only seems to look good when you are standing up!) Most times, I can't wait to get home and take that shit off!! It's like taking off your bra and setting the "girls" free at the end of the day, except I feel like a can of biscuits that just busted open!

Thank God it's only for special occasions because I can't see myself wearing that shit every day!

Diary Entry - January 6, 2016

Who in their right mind would wear white yoga pants? Unless you run every day, squat the fuck out of your glutes, quads and hammies *and* have good genetics and not an ounce of fat anywhere on your body, you're asking for punishment. Those bastards will hug and emphasize every nook and cranny on your fanny and everywhere in between. Kill me now for even attempting to try these on.....however my calves look amazing and was the perfect complement to my cottage cheese butt! Ugh....now excuse me while I make a liposuction appointment.

Diary Entry - December 28, 2015

This evening's train thought…...Why is bra shopping such a frustrating task? It should be pretty simple, right? One would think anyway. Nowadays you can order from your favorite websites but, if you are like me, you can't just order your size bra online and expect it to be perfect, even if the name supposedly "speaks for itself." Every bra is different and the bigger you are, the more difficult it is to find the "perfect" bra. And by perfect, I mean the right size, perfect support while lifting, separating and smoothing, yet still looking somewhat sexy. I'm in my 40's, I don't want to look like I am wearing my grandmother's bra. But unfortunately, even though they now make them look sexy in the bigger sizes, they still don't look sexy (in my opinion). I want to look like I am wearing a sexy bra, not a fucking tank top! I'm not THAT big, but big enough to have to try on nearly 50 bras to find the one bra that meets all my requirements, then just by a dozen in different colors! Boring! AND, at least for me, I can never find bottoms to match. Okay, so my OCD kicks in a little here and I'd like to coordinate! Oh shut up and stop shaking your heads, you ladies know you do it too, or at least try to, much like me!

My ideal bra would include:

- A perfect cup that lifts just enough and molds to your boobs, without gaps while not making you look like you have "torpedo tits" (Backstory: I had a co-worker years ago at my previous employer who walked around with her pointy tits high and proud, and we all used to laugh and we coined the phrase "torpedo tits"! Poor woman, I wonder how she's doing these days?).

- One that holds them up and in, with slight separation between the breasts creating a subtle cleavage, not a buttcrack cleavage.

- No double-bubble effect (aka a second set of boobs, or "piggyback" boobs), have a smoothing effect on the sides and back, thus eliminating back and side fat, and my biggest wish for the perfect bra.....

- Having straps just wide enough and cushioned enough to eliminate the shoulder indentations.

I know I have high expectations, so I'm sure during the course of my lifetime, I will never find "the one." I've tried those ones from the infomercials - pfffft....don't waste your money ladies! What poor excuses for a bras! They look more like an ugly sports bra and has little-to-no-support and does nothing that it claims to do!

I know some ladies will appreciate this humor. Sometimes I think humor is the only thing that gets us through the frustration. OK, rant over....carry on!

Diary Entry - December 18, 2015

Ok people listen up or tune out because I'm about to drop a few F-bombs and a few choice, unladylike words (shocker!) People with wheeled luggage during rush hour during the holidays are total douche biscuits! It's already bad enough that you're wheeling around your shit, but you can't be weaving in and out of people running for the train, then have the fucking nerve to get pissed off when someone trips and falls on your bag and bends the handle AND causes you to miss your train.

Listen up you little asshole, if you left a little earlier you wouldn't be running for the train and become a hazard to all the other folks around you. Have some courtesy and respect instead of acting like a little prick!

Merry Christmas, dickhead!   I hope Santa leaves you a giant ass so you can stuff yourself inside of it where you belong!

Diary Entry - November 30, 2015

People are quirky and I find myself watching them more and more. This morning on the train, I was watching a guy blow his nose, then he proceeds to examine its contents with each blow (why do people do this? It's gross, lol!) And not only did he examine it, he then shoved the tissue up both nostrils and gave it a twist. OK, I get that part. You wanna make sure you clear all the bats from the cave. He then takes out a plastic baggie from his backpack and places the used tissue in it – also totally fine. But then proceeds, ever so delicately, to tie this baggie into a double knot. Umm, why?? It's not going to explode its contents all over your bag or anyone else! Whatever…. So then a few moments later, I'm watching him again as he's picking the little lint balls from his coat in an OCD fashion and making sure that when he drops them on the floor, they don't attach to his pants or his shoes. OK so he's an OCD neat freak. But at the same time, his shoes are dirty and loosely tied, and his pants are a wrinkled mess. His behavior just struck me as odd. Lord only knows who's out there examining my quirkiness!

Diary Entry - September 16, 2015

Those who know me know that I have a voice for each of my animals. Meaning, if they could actually talk, it's what their voice would sound like, kind of like cartoon characters. So, not only do I have a voice for my pets but I have conversations with them in their voices and I answer them in my own voice. I also sing/meow/woof songs to them. For example, (sung to the tune of "All Star" by Smashmouth.) <clears throat…. ahem>…."Hey now, you're a kitty, get your meow on, go purr!"

OK, this could be the start of a serious psychological disorder.....

Diary Entry – June 23, 2015

Everyone has a stride when they walk right? I just lost my shit on some douchebag who just had to cut in front of me with his rolling backpack which caused me to trip and fall onto it and he has the fucking nerve to say "What the fuck?" to me!! And rather than helping me up, he stepped to the side and is bitching about his now broken handle. Newsflash, dickhead, you are not the only one trying to get to work! I'm glad I broke your fucking bag! Have a little respect and decency to apologize, fucker! It's your fault that your bag is broken!

Thank you to the gentleman who helped me up and offered to carry my bag for me while I limped for the next block to my office. Thank god there are still some decent people in this world.

Diary Entry - June 18, 2015

So to add to my commuter "chronicles", this morning's commute was kind of funny. And if you know me well, you'll know that even at my age, I still find this shit hilarious. Sitting on the train this morning, playing my usual games and checking social media (shut up, we all do it!) There were delays due to signal problems so of course the train is packed, asshole to elbow. Now we are nearly out of the tunnel and pulling into World Trade when the train stops, conductor announces that we're being held by the train's dispatcher and to please be patient. I continue to play my game and the rather large guy to my right spills his coffee all over the floor next to me and bends over and sifts through his backpack for napkins to clean it up. So I look over to see how he's making out and BAM... buttcrack everywhere! Ugh!

Meanwhile, the woman to my left is getting annoyed that she can't get a signal on her phone (duh lady, you can't get a signal inside a tunnel, dumbass!). It was bad enough that I had to listen to her yelling into her phone for almost the entire trip so I was glad when the call got lost. Anyway, out of nowhere, this thunderous fart vibrates the seat under us! I look up at my husband, who was standing in front of me, and watched his eyes widen as his lips mouthed "OMG!" He looked to the guy on my right, who also looked up at him and then he looks to the woman to my left who isn't even paying attention and is now shaking her phone. Then he smiled and says, "Wow, that's amazing!" Hahaha!

Care to guess which one dropped the bomb? And I mean, it was a BOMB!! Yep, the lady! And she didn't care one bit that people were looking at her. I couldn't contain my laughter (and I am loud when I laugh). Then I could see her turning red in the face as she scooted over one seat, then two seats, as people started to stand to get off the train.

Diary Entry - October 17, 2014

Making a mental list of the things that pissed me off today:

1. While running for the elevator this morning, I'm behind a guy (who doesn't see or hear me, apparently) as we move into the elevator, he lets one rip right in front of me and steps in with like 10 other people and we all had to suffer in his stench until I got off at the 45th floor - gross, dude!

2. I have not only the coffee-slurping douche sitting behind me, I now have another one sitting to my left. I could be mistaken but at one point I thought I heard them slurping in sync! To top it off, the guy next to me is

a loud chewer which sounds like a cartoon character chewing bubble gum!

3. While on the train this evening, I'm sitting across from this older, frumpy-looking guy who seems to be stuck in his rock star youth. He's playing air guitar with his right hand while reading his iPad and listening very loudly to rock music through his oversized, expensive headphones (well, at least he has good taste in music). But the way he's moving his hands and fingers looks like he's air spanking rather than air guitar. Give it up, dude! Whether air spanking or air guitar, you look ridiculous! And no one is impressed with your expensive headphones!

Diary Entry - October 17, 2014

Boy did I pick the wrong train car to sit in tonight with a pounding headache - yep, a car with a couple of screaming little kids under the age of five while parents are screaming into their cell phones in another language. Come on people - control your kids and have some respect for other passengers and shut the fuck up! My heels are two seconds from coming off and flying toward the back of this train car!

Diary Entry - June 18, 2014

I'm listening to two guys talking in the seat in front of me as we waited for the people to finish boarding in Newark. They were in their early thirties, maybe. At first glance, both very good looking. Of course I'm eavesdropping and heard them speak ill of women they know. Then proceeded to eyeball every decent woman walking by them and making derogatory and sexual comments among themselves. I sink lower in the seat to remain unseen. It's no wonder that some women have low self-esteem when you have assholes like them making comments the way they were (and loud enough to be heard). Shut the fuck up you little douchebags - it's a totally unattractive quality to have and makes you appear as ugly as your comments!

Diary Entry - June 11, 2014

I'm sitting on the train this evening, totally exhausted, and the woman sitting next to me has the hiccups that sound like she swallowed a mouse.....or a small child. Totally cracking up right now!

Diary Entry - May 22, 2014

So I'm a ride person. I love roller coasters and superfast, thrilling rides. I remember as a kid going to Great Adventure and standing in lines forever to get on Freefall. Sitting in that car with a friend and two other strangers, heart pounding with excitement and scared to death as the car suddenly jerked upward, to the top and you could see the entire amusement park. The car slowly moves forward and stops for a moment.....I'm dying of anticipation and suddenly....BUZZ!

The car drops and my stomach is suddenly in the back of my throat throwing punches at my uvula and saying, "Motherfucker, you had cheese fries and a shake for lunch, put me down!" Everyone screams. In three seconds you're at the bottom staring up at the sky and giggling...what a rush!

Now? Instead of screaming on any ride, I close my eyes and see how many times I can recite the Hail Mary before we take off and lucky if I don't pee my pants or paint the ride and its passengers with vanilla-coated cheese fries before those three seconds are over!

Still, what a rush! Good times!

Diary Entry - March 23, 2014

Who finds the smallest, slushy wet spot on a moving train and slips not once but TWICE?? Me! At least I got a few chuckles from fellow train riders (myself included) as they watched me slip n' slide down the aisle.

Diary Entry - March 17, 2014

Of course the one day I decide to drink a lot of water and then get on a train it just happens to be St. Patrick's Day and every restroom has a line of drunk hooligans waiting for it *or* it's out of order. Really??

Diary Entry - March 14, 2014

I'm listening to a flock of chicks on the train this morning because they are being so fucking loud at 7:00 am and interrupting my beauty sleep that I had no choice but to eavesdrop on their conversation. It amazes me how they speak, using the word "like" over and over again - ugh! So annoying - what are you a valley girl from the 80's? It's just as bad hearing a professional speaker use the word "umm" as a filler when delivering a speech. Oh, and I love how the sentence has an upward tick toward the end and sounds like it ends in a question. I zone in on that shit for some reason and shake my head.

Diary Entry - January 31, 2014

This guy gets on the crowded subway and stands directly in front of where I'm sitting. He puts his hands up to hold the bar above him. The zipper on his pants is unzipped and he's fucking commando - that's just perfect! 20 minutes on the train with this guy's junk in my line of sight! I can't unsee that!

I tried looking away but that would appear too obvious. I'm certain that the people to my immediate left and right saw his chubby love muscle too. I think it was flirting with me - I swear I saw it flex and blow kisses at me!

Diary Entry - July 16, 2013

Ladies, no matter how beautiful you are please remember it is *NOT* attractive to be fishing your shorts out of your crotch every 10 steps.

Here's a tip: If the shorts are too short or tight, perhaps this means you need a bigger pair! That is all...

Diary Entry - May 16, 2013

So I take a break from work grab my e-cig and head outside for a few minutes to enjoy some of this gorgeous day and of course, people watch! NYC is the best for this. During my 15 minute break I observed the following:

- Nearly 100 people talking on, texting or taking pics on their cell phone

- Two guys picking their nose

- Ten guys spitting (gross)

- Five guys crotch grabbing (some more than once!)

- Four girls picking their 'way too short' shorts out of their hineys (again, some more than once) and;

- One woman adjusting her boobs under her shirt in front of a deli window, while people sat there eating their lunch!

No one is perfect but really?? Some things are not meant for the public to see. Have some couth people! Didn't your mama teach you better than that??

Diary Entry - March 6, 2013

I know that working in New York City, you are subject to all the latest fashion trends, but, dudes in skinny jeans….. REALLY? Do I really need to go here? I know it's a trend and all, but what's worse are the dudes who wear the colored skinny jeans! Hey douche, are you wearing your sister's jeans?? Why don't you just put on a pair of spandex or yoga pants and be done already.

And by the way, your junk doesn't look any bigger, just sayin'.....

Diary Entry – January 10, 2012

So last night I stopped to get a cup of coffee. I didn't have pockets so I just shoved the change in my bra (come on ladies, I know you've *all* done this!) Totally forgetting I did this, I go home and change into a t-shirt and track pants and eventually lie down and fall asleep.

This morning I'm getting ready to shower and remove my clothes. I happened to glance in the mirror and the change (a quarter and a nickel) was still stuck to my left boob! I guess it gives new meaning to the words "treasure chest" ha ha!

Diary Entry – September 20, 2011

Random wonderings…. Why do women, while applying mascara, feel the need to open their mouth and stretch their cheeks? One thing has nothing to do with the other!! I guess they're attempting to catch flies while putting on make-up.

Diary Entry - August 18, 2010

I really dislike the word "like"! Seriously, have you ever listened to the way the younger generation speak and how many times they use the word "like" in one sentence? I tend to zone in on these annoying little things! It amazes me how these people got past a job interview and are out there working and communicating professionally.

Diary Entry - June 15, 2010

Tonight I had to stay at work late to work an event. Rather than taking a car home, I decided to take the train. As I sit in Penn Station as people board and fill the train, a group next of 20-somethings get on, clearly drunk. A girl sits behind me and I can hear the banter between her and her friends and the group of guys across the aisle. I think to myself "I'm so tired, I just want a little peace for this ride home."

The train begins to move and we are on our way. I hear some shuffling behind me and a guy sits down next to one of the girls. It's just the two of them in the seat now having a conversation. This guy, although buzzed, seems to have his shit together and has travelled a bit. Occasionally, I look at the reflection in the window as I look toward the seat behind me. I see the girl twirling her hair in a flirtatious manner and seems genuinely interested in their conversation. He began to tell her of the places he visited in the US and mentioned that one of his favorite places that he's visited was Alaska.

Girl: *"Alaska? Really? Isn't it like cold there with lots of snow?"*
Guy: *"No, not all the time. But I just happened to be up there at the time where the daylight period was short and the nights were really long. But I got to see the Aurora Borealis. And it was amazing. Have you ever seen the Aurora Borealis?"*
Girl: (giggling) *"No, what is that?"*
Guy: *"Really, you've never heard of the Aurora Borealis?"*
Girl: *"Umm, isn't that just the fancy word for women's nipples?"*

I burst into laughter and their conversation suddenly paused for a moment. I shook my head as the tears rolled down my cheeks, trying to contain my laughter.

Guy: *"Uh, no. That would be the areolas"*
Girl: *"Ohhh!"*

Diary Entry - April 6, 2010

As I people watch on the bus ride home I ponder... How funny would it be to live in a world like dogs do, walking around all day sniffing people's butts. The mental picture is making me giggle!

Photo Credit: John Ahrens

Stick That in Your
Juice Box and Suck It!

So, as you know I am a lady with a perverted mind, and this chapter is all about sexual innuendos and perverted, yet funny thoughts, as I've seen them in my head. Those who follow me may have seen a lot of my antics on social media. Sometimes I wonder how this shit just rolls out of my mouth, or in this case, through my fingertips!

Over the years I have fallen victim to one too many "that's what she said" jokes, and in retrospect, I suppose they were funny. Hell, they are STILL funny! When I am around like-minded friends who get my sense of humor, there is no telling what will come out of our mouths, especially if wine is involved!

Diary Entry - September 13, 2018

I am going to admit something right here and now. I'm addicted to anything banana! Banana yogurt, banana ice cream, banana muffins, banana liquor, banana chips, banana smoothies, flaming bananas foster, chocolate-dipped frozen bananas, banana split with lots of whipped cream, banana taffy or candies, banana cream pie (ha, ha - "banana 'cream' pie" - yeah, go ahead and laugh at that one, cause if you have a perverted mind like me, I *KNOW* you went there too!) Banana hammock? (ha, ha - yeah, that too!) Oh, and I'll go bananas without the real, fresh banana! Maybe I should have been a monkey? Wait, no cause then I'd be spank--.......uhhh, nevermind. Umm, you know what? Don't answer that!

Diary Entry - April 12, 2018

The things I ponder during my commute......

Coccyx (pronounced "cock-six") also known as the tailbone. Hmm, let's think about this for a minute... The dude whose job it was way back in the day to give this part a name had to have had a GREAT sense of humor! Seriously, how ironic is it that this bone is located at the very bottom tip of the spine, pretty close to the anus (aka "the asshole" to those who don't know this term) P.S. also another funny word....heh, heh....anus. Oh the jokes that would derive from this region of the body with names like Coccyx or tailbone, located near the asshole. Hmm, do you think this dude liked anal? I mean there's just so many coincidences in naming these parts and their location on the body. I think he had one too many glasses of scotch while diagramming and got all flirty with his wife one night and started rattling off one-liners…..

"Hey baby, I'll give you a little bone in your tail!"

"Wanna touch my 'coccyx bone'?"

"Can I put my six-inch-cock (aka 'coccyx' or 'cock-six') in your asshole (aka 'anus')?"

"Honey, that's a great word, write that shit down!" She giggled.

Diary Entry - April 11, 2018

Men have testicles. So when people say to me, "Boy, for a woman you sure have some big balls!" My response: "I prefer to call them 'breasticles' and yes, they're pretty big!"

Diary Entry - April 4, 2018

Why do we pet the kitty, yet we spank the monkey? What did that monkey ever do to you that he deserves a spanking? Some spank that monkey several times a day. That's just plain cruel and animal control should be called on you! I pet my kitty all the time and she loves it! Maybe pet the monkey from head to tail using long, steady strokes? Your monkey might like that instead of a spanking!

Diary Entry - April 2, 2018

Is this Mother Nature and Old Man Winter's idea of an April fool's joke, a day late? This is my birthday month and I want flowers and warmth, dammit! Just stop messing around and fuck already, will ya??! I'm sick of all this white shit! The only white shit that should be spewing is........umm, yeah......I hate snow!

Diary Entry - March 27, 2018

My love......Your scent is intoxicating as I wrap my hands around you, snuggle up and feel your warmth around my fingers. You fill me with warm, creamy deliciousness from the moment you touch my lips and I smile as I savor every drop of you. You have no idea what you do to me but I know I can always count on you to keep me satisfied. Oh heavenly, delicious coffee....I love you!

What? You thought I was being perverted? Shame on you!

Diary Entry - March 23, 2018

I'm a little silly, mixed with a shot of perverted, a shot of funny, a shot of "don't fuck with me" and just a tiny dash of crazy. Shake me up and serve me in a tall glass garnished with a slice of sexy. Damn, ain't that one hell of a cocktail? I call it.....

"The Sandycaine" and it goes down nice and smooth......ahhhh!

Diary Entry - March 22, 2018

I know it's not summer yet but I have a craving for pistachio ice cream with whipped cream and cherries on top....ooooh butter pecan sounds oh so yummy too! I like nuts in my ice cream, is that wrong? Loaded with fucking whipped cream. Just squirt that shit on top, baby, drown it in whipped cream! I'll lick it all off! WTF is wrong with me?? Wait, what's wrong with *you* fuckers? I'm just talking about ice cream, you all took this to a whole new level! Bunch of perverts.....

Diary Entry - March 21, 2018

Hey snow, I call BULLSHIT! Fucking asshole snow! I waited all night for you to give me at least 11 inches! I even lit some candles, poured some wine, put on my best lingerie (yoga pants and t-shirt) and ya gave me a half inch?? What a letdown! Such a tease!

Diary Entry - March 18, 2018

I'm off to the dentist this evening but hey, I look forward to the drillin' & droolin' and I'm not even writing my naughty stuff! *"Oh yeah baby, bring it on! Give to me good! Right there, oh yeah, drill me good you sexy, oral-lovin' hussy!"*

I don't think the hygienist appreciates my perverted sense of humor, but at least I made her laugh! Xanax makes me funny! Who knew?

P.S. I literally just heard the dental assistant say, and I quote, *"I'm gonna put the oral in the front and the hygiene in the back."* Yes, I burst out laughing, but she was referring to the rooms! This is gonna be fun! Now, where's my laughing gas to make this visit complete?? HA!

Diary Entry - February 14, 2018

OK folks, Valentine's Day. We all know this is a made up holiday created as an excuse to woo your significant other with dinner, flowers, chocolate, and lingerie or power tools, whatever...... all this with the promise of nookie at the end of the night. And guys, we all know your woman will want you to wear that extra special, dental floss-enhanced cock sock she bought you last year. And rightfully so, this day only comes once a year, right? Hmm....who are we kidding here? They should just rename the holiday to Vaginatine's Day - now *that* would be a holiday worth celebrating! Screw Cupid and his stupid arrows, that flying baby is just creepy! Wouldn't you rather see a flying vagina? Wait......what? And yes, I said "nookie"......so bite me!

And, while you're planning the big night of bumpin' uglies, why not pick up a copy of **Bedtime Stories: His Words, Her Desires** for your sweetheart today. Go ahead, pick on me for using words and phrases from ages ago. But hey, at least you chuckled for a minute, no? Happy Vaginatine's Day! Now go have some fun!

Diary Entry - February 6, 2018

Have you ever bitten into a bad nut? Now, before all your perverted minds start to roll on the floor laughing, I'm talking about pistacios. Best nuts to eat while you're watching what you eat and balancing a healthy diet.

So, here I am on a roll, cracking them open, munching on nuts (yeah, OK I can see you all giggling right now - "hee, hee - she said 'munching on nuts'!") but seriously, I start my day off with nuts because of the protein (go ahead, chuckle at that one too!).

I love anything pistachio flavored (ice cream, gelato, pudding, cake - although I do not eat any of this right now - I substitute by eating the nut itself). This morning I was having my coffee and cracking open the shells, popping them into my mouth one after the other as I'm catching up on my morning routine at work.

Suddenly I bit into a really foul-tasting nut. Hey, it happens! I nearly vomited as I spit it out. I have people in and out of my office all morning long, it's my busiest time of the day. A fairly new, male co-worker walks in my office as I'm spitting said nut into the trash can next to my desk. Embarrassed, I say, "sorry, just had a bad nut!" Immediately, he bursts out laughing! Now, he's about 15 years younger than me and thinking about what I just said out loud to him, my face starts to get red hot and I feel the blood rushing to my cheeks.

Clearly, he should know I'm talking about nuts because the empty shells are on the napkin on my desk - but yep, he went right for the dirty thought! I guess I should watch how I phrase things, eh?

Diary Entry - June 25, 2017

I've said it before and I'll say it again. Chinese food.... Why must the broccoli in my chicken & broccoli be so damn big? I mean seriously, I need a fucking chainsaw to cut that shit up! Would it kill you to chop it up into manageable, bite-sized pieces? I don't want to look like I'm deep-throating a bonsai tree when I'm trying to eat my lunch in public for fuck's sake! I'm eating with chopsticks too, not a fork and knife in sight!

The looks on these people's faces as I look up from my dish like a chipmunk who just shoved a bunch of nuts in my cheek, is just fucking hilarious, yet embarrassing!

Thank god for napkins, as I quickly cover my mouth and try to chew like a lady!

Diary Entry – February 3, 2013

Ooooh baby...... I love to feel you in my hands as I take you in and feel your warmth against my lips and tongue as you slide down my throat and fill me with excitement and warmth. There's no one better than you. You're so good that I have to have you more than once. I love you coffee!

And there you go again, thinking perverted thoughts……sinners! 😜😜

Photo Credit: John Ahrens

Lewd, Crude and Just Plain Rude

There have been many times over the course of my career as an event planner where I have stayed in the City late for a work event, or happy hour with co-workers, or dinner with friends and family. These have been the times where I've experienced some of the unimaginable. When it's time to go home, there is a whole different cast of characters that frequent the late trains. They're usually drunk and extremely loud and half the time they fall asleep on the train and miss their stop. Horny, drunk frat boys groping their girlfriends on the train and dry humping in the seats. For the most part, during the normal commuting hours, I'm travelling with people who also commute to the City for work. Sometimes I am just baffled that some of the strangest people live so close to home!

Diary Entry - March 19, 2018

Typical conversation with myself while commuting.......

Me: "Quite frankly, I don't like your attitude!"
Me: "Really? Well, 'quite frankly', you can go fuck yourself!"

True story!

Diary Entry - March 25, 2016

I don't know what's worse, a guy adjusting his junk in his pants pocket, knowing there is limited movement in the pocket of those skinny jeans, and as a result is now making moves that can only be described as a combination of something that, judging by his reaction, just yanked out a stray pubic hair while doing the Irish jig......OR just flat out adjusting himself over his tight jeans for all to see. It was quite amusing to see the adjustment over the skinny jeans as he had a camel toe worse than any woman I've seen and he was only drawing more attention to that thing as he tried to move it, only for it to bounce right back into place like the Ball-in-a-Cup game. And if your Ker-Bangers are that big, why the fuck would you wear skinny jeans? It's not a fashion statement you ballsy douche! You look dumb and just as bad as a chick in low rise jeans with a muffin top. Put some on some 505's already and set those boys free!

Diary Entry - January 7, 2016

My daily rant about nothing, yet something. Sometimes I wish I had my own sitcom to bring these posts to life. Honestly, they are quite hilarious the way I envision them in my head, and I'm hoping that by my descriptive imagination, you can see the whole picture too. That said, why is it that men can shove their hand down their pants to adjust or scratch themselves and this is considered normal or acceptable behavior? I see a lot of this. Yet, if a woman does the same (not like we have anything to adjust, just saying for comparison purposes) its considered gross? Hey, sometimes there's a stray pube that gets caught in the lace of our panties and gets pulled – then the physical reaction is quite funny because most women will NOT shove their hand down their pants or up their skirt to adjust but rather do a funny little move or dance to try and wiggle it free. Ladies, this doesn't always work – trust me, I've been there. Simple solution – wax that shit or go commando! And don't give me that "It's Winter, I don't do hair removal in Winter, blah blah blah," just DO IT! And guys, I know you all have a million excuses for why you do this, but for the love of Pete, can you please at least try to be inconspicuous about it? How can you walk down a crowded street and do this in front of hundreds of people, looking like you're trying to straddle a horse, and not be embarrassed? (notice that I said "straddle" a horse, not to be confused with you're hung like a horse and that's the reason you make those silly moves). I mean I understand the whole ball thing sticking to your leg and all but here's a solution for you – how about using some baby powder with cornstarch? It's refreshing, keeps you somewhat dry and has a pleasant odor – just sayin'.

Diary Entry – September 15, 2015

As the seasonal summer comes to an end, I start to change up my wardrobe and make-up accordingly (close-toed shoes, darker lipstick, light sweater for the chilly mornings, etc.) On the walk up to my office this morning, I passed a security guard manning one of the little stations near the 9/11 memorial. He joked and asked me if he could trade his half cup of coffee for my full cup. I smiled and said that I wish I could but that I need the caffeine today. He gave me a rather scary look and didn't say another word. As I got in the elevator in my building, I smiled and said good morning to a couple of ladies that work on my floor. They gave me a strange look too!

So now I'm thinking, "WTF? Does my breath smell? Are my boobs popping out of my top? Is there something in my teeth?" Now panicked, I get off the elevator and run to the ladies room to see what was up. Looked at my smile and noticed deep red lipstick all over my teeth - looked as if I had bitten someone! I can see how that would make someone look at me strangely. Hahaha!

But ladies, help a sister out and tell me if I have lipstick on my teeth!

Diary Entry - August 10, 2015

I was on the fence about this but now I officially 100% HATE those damn selfie sticks and the assholes that use them. Tonight when walking to the train, I crossed Church Street at Vesey Street and for those who know or work in the area know that it is jam packed with people at rush hour. A group of girls are walking toward me and one chick has her shorts so far up her crotch I thought I saw Camel Joe winking at me. And there she is walking and twirling her hair with her selfie stick out in front of her, not paying attention and nearly missing my eye by a couple of inches. And she had the nerve to shoot me a dirty look because I tapped the stick trying to dodge her as she walked by. Dumb bitch does not know who she's messing with!

Stupid selfie stick......

Diary Entry – March 3, 2015

I've had some weird shit happen to me while commuting over the years but tonight's tops the cake. It's bad enough that I had to work late in this shitty weather, with Path train delays but I managed to get to Newark in time for my train (which is not my normal train and it's packed full of assholes) but luckily I found a seat to myself. I'm only seated a few minutes and checking work emails when suddenly I hear this heavy breathing from behind me, almost as if someone was sleeping. I look to my left to catch his reflection in the window to find him standing over me from the back and sniffing deeply at the top of my head!! Are ya fucking kidding me?? I pull away and yell, "WTF? Weirdo!" And I quickly find a new seat. No wonder that seat was empty on a crowded train!

I hope you got a good whiff, ya freak! Eww!!

Diary Entry – June 26, 2014

I'm waiting in the lobby of my building this morning, waiting for my elevator. I hear the ding of the bell that one of the six elevators has arrived. I make my way toward the opening doors when out of nowhere, this girl cuts me off, nearly tripping me to get in the elevator and doesn't even apologize (stupid bitch). The elevator is express to my floor on 45. She's going to 53, the top floor. The elevator doors open on 45 and get off, but not before I swipe my hand down all the remaining buttons as I step out, forcing her to stop at every floor from 46 to 53!

Yep, I'm that bitch! The look on her face as the doors closed was priceless!

Diary Entry - May 6, 2014

A woman was getting off the train tonight and decides to step in the aisle right in front of me and backs up stepping so hard on my toe that she cracked my toenail! So I kicked her. Is that mean?

Diary Entry - January 31, 2014

A guy gets on the subway and stands in front of where I'm sitting. He puts his hands up to hold the bar above him. Without really thinking, I zone in on his crotch. The zipper on his pants is unzipped and he's commando! That's just fucking perfect, 20 minutes on the train with this guy's junk in my line of sight! I can't unsee that!

Diary Entry - August 13, 2013

It's about a quarter mile walk from the train station to my building in a downpour, sloshing through puddles and dodging umbrellas as people quickly brush past me in the opposite direction. While the crowd waited for the light to change so that we can cross the street, a woman behind me decided to shake the excess water from her umbrella right down my back! Then to add insult to injury a bus speeds by along the curb splashing us all! Since I'm already soaked and my umbrella no longer serves a purpose, what do I do? I laugh loudly and hysterically like a psycho and start stomping my feet in the puddles.

I'm sure those people were not happy but none of them said a word! They must have thought I was crazy. But that's nothing new to New Yorkers, everyone is a bit nutty these days!

Diary Entry - June 23, 2013

Tonight's train commute was rather quiet, I was quite surprised that the usual suspects on the train were not as loud and obnoxious as they normally were. However the train was crowded. I was sitting in an aisle seat where I would normally occupy a window seat. I looked around the seats in my immediate surroundings and most were sleeping, reading or looking at their phones. I caught sight of a guy about five seats ahead of me and on the opposite side of the aisle, and facing me. He occupied the seat directly next to the door and was sitting alone. I noticed that he had taken his shoes off, which I found quite odd because he didn't have socks on and the floors on the train are absolutely disgusting! I examined his appearance (what else is new, I was bored and what else was I going to do for the next hour on a quiet train car?).

The man was asleep and his head was tilted to one side and he was sort of slumped down in the seat, legs spread wide. He wore baggy shorts, a little shorter that I would have expected for a guy of his age (which was somewhere around early-forties). Something caught my attention and not having my glasses on and being able to see clearly, I fumbled through my purse for my phone, and I very subtly took his picture. I zoomed in on the pic and was mortified! His junk was peeking out through the bottom of his shorts! I immediately looked at him again because I was in disbelief, only this time, I got caught looking! My face turned beet red and I turned into the seat so that I was out of his eyesight and so that I could hide my embarrassment. I still had the pic open on my phone as the conductor crept up behind me and had his head over my shoulder.

"So what are we looking at?" He whispered, with his head right next to my ear. I had become friendly with the conductor who worked those three train cars on that particular train every night. We'd always joke around and I found him to be funny, yet really obnoxious. Not wanting him to think I was a pervert (ha!), I tried to close the picture but it was too late.

"Oh I see you've finally met Ballsy," he said, with utter sarcasm in his voice.

"Excuse me?" I replied, clearly still red in the face and beginning to sweat.

"That guy always has his junk hanging out. He sits in that spot on purpose because he faces the rest of the people on the train. Did he catch you looking?" He said with a humorous smile.

"Uhh, oh my God, yes he did! I can't even look at that guy ever again. Do you think he knows I was looking?" I asked him.

"Probably, that's his intention," he said, as he laughed at me. "Look at you, all embarrassed and shit!"

"Shut the fuck up and go away, will you? I've got an unintentional naughty picture I need to delete right now."

Diary Entry - June 21, 2013

Hey train douche! Thanks for leaving your size 22 foot in the aisle for me to trip over in my open toe heels and break my toenail. A simple "sorry" would have been nice but you were too busy talking on your phone and couldn't muster up those words but instead look annoyingly down at your own foot to see any damage I might have caused. Hey fucker, my dainty size 8 did nothing to your Neanderthal foot yet my toe is a bloody mess. Thanks a lot asshole!

Diary Entry - January 30, 2013

The guy sitting next to me on the train keeps doing the "pinch n' roll" - ugh! Guys, I know you know this but for the ladies, if you don't know this move, it's a guy's way of scratching his balls without actually scratching them (pinching the scrotum and rolling it between their fingers). Ya know, if women did that we'd be looked at with disgust!

Diary Entry - April 9, 2013

I was being nosey on the train and looking over some dude's shoulder across the aisle to see him opening up pictures of girls on some dating website and zooming first on her chest, then ass, then legs and finally her face. I see where HIS priorities are! Then I got busted looking! Hahaha!

Diary Entry – November 10, 2012

This morning's commute was rather annoying. With the trains still not running to the City due to the aftermath of superstorm Sandy (yep, I cause trouble wherever I go - ha ha!), I was forced to take the bus which was packed with people who would normally commute by train. I used to commute by bus in my early days, but had switched to the train back in 2009. I prefer to sit in the window seat so I find one open window seat next to a man. I politely ask him if I can sit so he gets up to let me in. I settle into the seat and we are on our way.

Within a few minutes, this guy falls asleep and his legs are spread apart, invading my space. His whole body is relaxed and he's now leaning on me. I tried to move as close to the window as possible to give myself more room but that didn't work, he just spread himself out further. Now, I'm trying to nudge him to wake him up so that he can adjust himself in the seat. That didn't work either! Now his mouth is open and I can smell his nasty morning breath – gross! Why do guys have to manspread so much? You're junk ain't that big that it warrants you to take up a seat and a half on the bus! I've sat next to rather large people on the bus that take up less room than you! Have some consideration and close your legs, fucker!

Diary Entry - July 13, 2011

Why do men feel the need to adjust & scratch their manparts in public? The train is full of men moving their crotch around, and for those who commute by subway know how crowded the trains get. I don't wanna see some dude fondling his junk in front of me while I sit! It's already bad enough that we sit at the perfect "blowjob height" on the subway but don't make it any more uncomfortable for us. How would you react if a woman decided to scratch her ladyparts in public?

Not a sexy visual, is it?

Photo Credit: Sandy C. Jayne

Just Because…
Purely Fucked Up and Pretty Funny Shit!

A very dear friend of mine with a sense of humor much like mine, let's just call her "Ana" (ha, ha!), suggested that in addition to my random thoughts, rants and commuter stories, that I include for you some very funny stories from way back and some funny things that are even more recent. Why you ask? Well, just because! These are not all commuting related but still pretty funny. Don't judge, just have a laugh. Though some of you may not get my sense of humor, I know many, if not most of you, can relate to at least one of these stories.

Diary Entry – December 5, 2018

I've been a busy bee lately but I know you all miss my silly shenanigans! I'm about to tell you a pretty personal story of a very recent experience and you will either relate and laugh, or find me completely appalling - and if the latter, well then hey, I apologize and hopefully Santa brings you a sense of humor for Christmas!

We all get to a point in our lives, usually at a later age, where we start to realize that our bodies don't function as well as they used to, or bounce back from trauma as quickly as we once did. Shit sags, little aches and pains here and there, wrinkles, a little weight gain, and quite a few grays in the mane. It's all part of aging gracefully, as they say. And at some point we start going to the doctor a little more frequently. Recently, I have had some issues with heartburn and acid reflux and pain in my stomach so I decided it was time to see a gastro doc. With insurance nowadays it seems to take MORE time than it used to in order to get a referral or an appointment and oftentimes it takes three visits to finally get a test done. What a pain in the ass and a waste of my time and money!

Anyway, I start by going to my general practitioner. She then referred me to a couple of different gastro doctors. Being that my insurance company is so damn inconvenient, I needed to call them first to see A. if I needed a referral, and B. to see if a particular doctor within that group took my insurance (just because it's a group, doesn't necessarily mean that the doctor themselves participate).

So after that pain in the ass inconvenience, I also learned that all of what I was about to endure was going to come out of my own pocket, until I've reached my deductible of $2500. What in the fuck?? What normal, healthy person meets that deductible in a calendar year?? Annoyed, but moving on!

I finally secure an appointment for the gastro doctor. I go in, he interviews me, asks me a buttload of personal questions about my poop history in addition to my acid reflux problems. He examined me for all of 5 seconds as he poked and prodded my sore abdomen (the initial reason for my visit because I thought I might have a gall bladder or appendix issue). He says he wants to do some tests - blood work, ultrasound, endoscopy and a colonoscopy. Now, in my head I am seeing multiple appointments that I'll need to take days off for, or leave early from work, etc. and I see the dollar signs adding up. But alas, health is the most important issue here! So he types up in his little laptop and tells me that I can see the woman outside to schedule my appointment.

Curious I asked, "Appointment? Don't I need *multiple* appointments for these procedures?" He replied, "Nope, we can do the endoscopy and colonoscopy at the same time. But I won't be performing the procedure, my colleague will."

Now I panic at the thought of having a tube up my ass and another down my throat and people peering at my insides. But wait, do they actually perform them at the same time? And if they don't, I have to make sure that they don't stick a shitty tube down my throat. Oh no, what if they get so busy that they fuck that all up and I wake up with shit breath? Wait, I wake up with shit breath anyway! Doesn't everyone? Oh, and I had to call the insurance company AGAIN to see if the doctor performing the procedure accepts my insurance. Another pain in the fucking ass!

So I make the appointment for the endoscopy and colonoscopy for exactly a week later and the scheduler gives me a ton of crap to read. I hate to read anything medical related, even if it is for my OWN health! No offense to my friends in the medical profession - much love and respect to you for taking good care of me, I know my ass is in good hands - literally! Not knowing what I was in store for, I had these images in my head of having a tube up my ass and another down my throat at the same time and I couldn't help but see myself as nothing more than a sliding charm on a Pandora bracelet! (yeah, picture that!!) Ugh, I hoped that wasn't the case because I was a virgin to these procedures!

The paperwork included a bunch of scripts for ultrasound, blood work, acid reflux medication and literature on why the fuck I need to have these tests in the first place. Then there is this thing they called SUPREP. Which, my dumb ass read it quickly and referred to as Super Prep - like this thing was so powerful it was going to make my ass explode or something. To my surprise, it was 2 six ounce bottles to be diluted and consumed about 10 hours apart (at least for me, that was the instruction I was given a few days before the "procedure").

I had heard from many friends and family who have had the procedure done that the "prep" was the worst part. Prep?? What prep?? There is no fucking prep for this thing!! You can't prep for doing anything but staying within 10 feet from the bathroom for the next 18 hours!

I consumed nothing but clear liquids and orange jello the next day, until it was time for me to take my Super Prep (ha!). I opened the bottle and smelled it. It sort of smelled like a weird fruit punch so how bad could it possibly be, right? I dilute it in a cup with 10 ounces water and I take a sip…

Holy - fucking - shit!!

That motherfucker tickled my gag reflex instantly and started throwing sucker punches at my uvula! That was the nastiest shit I have ever consumed! And I still had another 15 ounces to drink. How the hell was I going to do that? This stuff tasted like those barrel fruit punch drinks with the tinfoil tops that we used to love to drink as a kid - but mixed with some sort of salty solution. I gagged painfully with each sip and tried my best to keep it from coming back up. It was so fucking nasty that I had to pinch my nose closed and go for the chug to minimize the amount of times I was going to taste that putrid shit.

Let's fast forward to just about the 29 minute mark from the first sip...... You can kinda guess where this is going right? Ha ha! Well, I felt the uncomfortable sensation settle into my lower bowel and I made a mad dash for the bathroom.

What I can say about this instance and the 30 other instances that followed every 20 minutes, is that although I needed to be close to the bathroom, I didn't have the insane sweats or cramping that I expected when I was told "the prep is the worst part." This might be TMI but after the first few times, it began to flow like water out of my butt - which was the weirdest sensation. Oh - and for the love of God, never, and I mean NEVER, EVER trust a fart!!

After about the 30th time, I was finally able to get some sleep, woke up early and decided to do the prep a half hour earlier than they had originally told me to. Because, knowing me and how I reacted to it the day before, I was not looking forward to doing it again and I knew it was going to take me a few extra minutes to get that shit down. I'm crabby as fuck and all I really wanted was a cup of coffee, not this nasty, salty, fruit punch-flavored ass blaster I was consuming. And it was a good thing that I did take it early, because I was in that bathroom up until 10 minutes before my appointment. Talk about cutting shit close! Literally!!

Two things I highly recommend getting, based on my experience in the "prep" is this:

1. Butt wipes
2. Vaseline

Because your ass is going to be raw and sore from all that wiping! Buy them, use them and love them!!! They will be your best friend for those 24 hours. Oh, and invest in some quality TP, not the cheap shit. Your butt with thank you! I wish I had known this much earlier than I did. I walked into my appointment like someone had shoved a dry stick up my ass without the benefit of a little A&D and a glass of wine!

Now it's time for my procedure. I speak with the anesthesiologist, sign the consent forms and off I go. They roll me into a room where there is a nurse, the doctor and her assistant. Doctor and nurse were female, the assistant was a male. A young, 30-something, attractive male. Are ya fucking kidding me right now?? Not that I should care at my age, and I should be happy that I am being proactive about my health - but shit, I am naked from the waist down under this flimsy hospital gown and I am about to be put under anesthesia for the next 40 minutes. Who knows what the assistant's job is and I didn't really have time to ask questions as the nurse was prepping my arm to administer the needle with the sleepytime medicine.

All that was going through my mind at this point was, "is this guy gonna be spreading my buttcheeks apart as the doctor inserts the tube and camera into my ass?" 😨😨😨 What a shitty job for him - hahaha!

I make a few nervous, and inappropriate jokes about being taken out to dinner first, which made them all laugh and kind of put my mind at ease about what was about to happen. The assistant then tells me he's going to put a mouth guard in my mouth to help hold it open for the endoscopy tube.

I can't really talk at this point and the nurse says, "OK, I'm going to administer the anesthetic now." I didn't really have time to acknowledge her as I blinked once or twice and I was out.

I woke up in recovery which seemed like it was just a few short minutes later, and the reason I woke up is because I was farting uncontrollably! 🌀🌀🌀 I couldn't even try to be quiet or ladylike about it! And of course, where they left me was right in front of the nurse's station where medical staff were walking by constantly.

One of the nurses stopped by and asked me a few questions about how I was feeling. I actually felt fine, good in fact. She adjusted the bed to sit me up but before doing so she said to me, "it's okay if you pass gas, everyone does and it's perfectly normal. It's because of the air they put into your colon in order to do the test."

As she adjusted the bed I used my stomach muscles to help lift myself up which forced the air out even harder and my butt sounded like a machine gun! I burst out laughing which made the sound louder and in sync with my obnoxiously, loud belly laugh! I laughed so hard I was in tears - and it just kept coming. I contained my laughter to more of a raspy giggle as the tears rolled down my face. I could hear the people on the other side of the curtain on either side of me laughing along with me. Here I am, 47 years old and I'm giggling like a child. The nurse tried not to laugh but she couldn't help herself. Farts are funny, I don't care how old you are! And when they happen in embarrassing situations, it makes it that much more funny!

And there you have it folks - my fully-detailed colonoscopy/endoscopy experience! And yes, I do talk about the things that happen that no one likes to discuss. But hey, we are all human! If you can't laugh at yourself, then who can you laugh at? In this instance, you can laugh at me – it's quite alright! I'm happy to report that there are no serious issues with my digestive system and I don't have to go back until the ripe, young age of 50!

Diary Entry – July 13, 2018

Some trends I just don't understand. While I get that people wanna do piercings but what is with the guys and the earlobe stretching thing? Seriously? Between that and the doucheknot on top of your head you look like a real tool! What happens when you're 60, 70, 80? You'll have these giant, wrinkley, flabby earholes. AND I've seen people start doing this in their cheeks, exposing their teeth!!! Again, when you're old and you're eating, I don't need to see your ABC food coming out of your flabby cheekhole! Ewww! What if when you're sleeping, a bug crawls in there – OMG gross!

Face it, you look dumb!. Personally, I think it's gross to look at. What about now, what if you had a job interview? That shit won't get you a job, butt nugget! Hey, here's a FABULOUS idea....Why don't you use that same ring and stretch out your asshole. This way it will be much easier for you to shove your head up there for making a dumbass mistake!

Diary Entry – May 24, 2018

Manbuns..... I just want to take a second to talk about these. Every single dude I've ever met that has one of these has been a total douchebag. Which is why I like to call them "douche knots". I am really curious to know what goes through a guy's mind when he decides that that's the hairstyle he wants. Like does he wake up one day and say "I'm going to grow my hair out so that I can pull it back in a bun. I am going to look sooo cool and all

the women will want me. I am going to get laid!"
Maybe I'm just old but dude, seriously? All I want
to do when I see one of those fucking things is run
up behind you with a fucking giant pair of hedge
trimmers and cut that shit off!

It's not attractive, trust me. And when you
pair that hairstyle with skinny jeans, you look like
you just raided your sister's wardrobe. Just stop it
already, you look like a fucking tool!

Diary Entry - January 5, 2016

So those who know my tooth drama over the
last couple of weeks, here's a story that will either
make you laugh or scare the shit out of you anti-
dentist pussies (like me!).

I cracked a front tooth on New Year's Eve and
had to wait nearly a week to get an appointment and
suffered with this tooth pain and babying the shit
out of it to make sure it didn't fall out. I finally get
my appointment and get there and the doc asked me
when the last time I was at the dentist.

Feeling quite embarrassed, I said....

"Ummm, like 16 years ago." He looked at me, stunned.

His jaw dropped and he was shaking his head. And you there? Yes, *YOU* reading this, stop shaking your head too! I know I'm an anti-dentist pussy (as I stated above) and here is the reason why. 18 years ago I had three wisdom teeth pulled all at the same time because you know, I'm a superhero and I can handle any kind of pain (my stomach turned just saying that!) This dentist had the worst bedside manner. When he was working in my mouth, he reeked of cigarettes and had the worst breath. How the hell does a dentist have bad breath??

Anyway, the first two came out easy. As he pulled the last tooth, he was having some difficulty and he was cursing (he was seriously dropping F-bombs) that it wasn't coming out the way he wanted it to. No one wants to hear a fucking F-bomb when you're slightly sedated and he's yanking shit out of your mouth! When he finally got a good hold on that tooth and pulled, he dropped that fucker right on my chest! After realizing he did so, all he could say was "whoops!" as he quickly scooped up that bloody fang off my chest.

Talk about having the shit scared out of you and nearly vomiting at the same time! After he finished and cleaned me up, took the nitrous oxide off and I started to return to a less sedated phase, he comes back in with a little plastic bottle with all 3 wisdom teeth in it and asked me if I wanted to keep them - those fuckers were two inches long!! That was enough for me not to go back for a long time.

Let's fast forward two years from then. I needed a root canal on my front tooth but I had no dental insurance at the time. The work needed to be done and I paid out-of-pocket for it but at the time, could not afford the $1,500 for the porcelain crown so he put in a post and patched up my tooth and sent me on my way. A year later I had a car accident where I smacked my face on the steering wheel and weakened the tooth even further (shut up, I wasn't wearing my seat belt. I know, duh, so bite me!)

I survived the next 16 years until New Year's Eve where I bit into a bagel and cracked the tooth. I have gone to the dentist three times already and I am still not done. I loved this guy but he was another one with terrible bedside manner. He kept calling me "boss". As he's working on my teeth, he's using the drill and grinding the shit out of my teeth, water is splashing everywhere, all over my glasses, down the side of my face around the back of my neck and yes, even down the front of my shirt in my cleavage. I had to stop him at some point because I was soaked.

I said to him, "I appreciate what you're doing to help get my tooth fixed but do I smell bad?" He gave me a perplexed look.

"I thought I showered already before I came here," I said, with a bit of sarcasm. We had a good laugh and he was back to work. Only now I'm draped in paper towels all around my head, back of my neck and across my chest. I don't ever remember the water on those drills being so intense and drenching me. Anyway, he tried to put in a post and it snaps so he takes it out and he's drilling some more and says to me,

"Wait a minute, you already have a post there. I can see it, but that one is also broken so I have to take it out and put in a new one."

I nod as his hands are in my mouth so I clearly cannot speak. Then he says….ready for this???

"Well this is gonna have to come out now," as he snapped off my tooth with his fingers!! Oh my God, the horror!! Immediately the tears began to roll down my face (as if my face wasn't wet enough already). He stops, sits me up and says,

"Don't worry, I am not going to leave you like this. It's OK, I will make it look beautiful, I promise!" My response....

"See, this is why I haven't gone to the dentist in 16 years. You got any drugs or gas you can give me, perhaps a Xanax?" Again, we laughed.

"Hahahaha, I'm not kidding," I said, with as a straight a face as I could muster, considering the amount of Novocain in my mouth, which was quite funny in itself. I caught a glimpse of myself in the mirror that he mistakenly left in my lap as we were having this conversation. I'll save the details on my other visits for another story.

The moral of this story is not to wait 16 years to go to the dentist. Don't be a pussy, just do it!

Diary Entry - February 15, 2018

Broke a tooth on Friday, couldn't get an appointment until last night to get it fixed. Aside from an emergency visit two years ago, I hadn't been to the dentist in 17 years. Find out last night after 18 x-rays (yes, 18 because they had no x-rays for me since it had been 17 years and everything is much different now and they needed my whole mouth done). Now, I wasn't in any pain when the tooth broke, nor after (and I swallowed that piece of tooth with my lunch that day!)

"Unfortunately your tooth is weak because you have some decay in the root, you need a root canal," the doctor said, behind his surgical mask.

I panicked because I hear nothing but horror stories from people about root canals. But I needed to get it done so that I can get my tooth fixed and be normal again. He numbs me up with so much Novocain that my face felt like it had blown up to 10 times its size and that I looked like a chipmunk after shoving lots of nuts in its cheek. My nose was numb, my lips were numb, my whole tongue was numb and all the way up the side of my face and down into my neck.

"Are ya feeling any numbness yet?" The doctor asked.

"Doc, I feel like I look like the Elephant Man, can we please get on with this?" I said, with a severe lisp as the drool starts to spill out the sides of my mouth and down my chin. (I soooo wished I had a mirror to see what I felt and how I must have looked!)

The doctor started the work, I hear and feel the drills in my mouth as the sound is amplified in my ears through my mouth. I cringe as the goosebumps start to form on the back of my neck and the tears started to roll from my eyes. The suction hose that was in my mouth to catch excess drool, had dried up my mouth so much that my lips were now sticking to the top and bottom teeth.

The doctor sees the tears running down my face and says,

"Are you ok, do you need a break? I know it's a lot and it takes a while," he said, as he sat me up and took the suction straw out of my mouth. "Here, why don't you rinse your mouth out and sit for a minute," he said, as he handed me a Dixie cup of water.

As I sat up, I caught a glimpse of myself in the small mirror on the wall next to the spit sink. I looked and felt like a character from In Living Color, Fire Marshall Bill (if you don't know who that is, YouTube him!) I swirled that shit around in my mouth like nobody's business and, forgetting how numb I was, the water trickled out the sides of my mouth and all down the front of me. Mind you, I had to stop several times as once the tooth was open, he had to shove these long-ass needle/screw-looking things into my tooth where he proceeded to twist and saw! Again I cringed and clenched my hands, digging my nails into the armrests of the chair and I squirmed like Zombie having an orgasm!

Let's jump ahead to where he's now putting a temporary filling on the tooth until I can come back next week to get a post, core and fitted for the crown. From behind me I see him burning some shit with a miniature blowtorch and proceeds to put that fucker right in my mouth! WTF?? Was he soldering my tooth? Anyway, we finish up and I can feel that I am still completely numb on the whole left side of my face and I had been in that office for two fucking hours!

"Take three Advil before that Novocain wears off so you are not in any discomfort," he said, as he took the bib off of my chest. Discomfort is an understatement! This fucker feels like the Devil himself took refuge in my molar and is digging in his pitchfork and laughing!

This morning I thought maybe, just maybe, the pain was finally gone. I baby-ed the fuck out of it and decided I would only eat on the right side of my mouth.

Well...........Holy Mother of God did I make a BIG mistake as I moved that granola bar accidentally to the other side of my mouth and chewed as I normally would. The pain brought tears to my eyes and a shriek to my lips as I screamed bloody hell! What in the fucking fuck was that?? Is it still supposed to hurt this much the next day? I'm actually afraid of my mouth right now, I think it might actually try to kill me!

So what's the good news after all this? I had no cavities - not one! Go me! But fuck me sideways, that bitch hurt!!

Diary Entry - November 10, 2015

This is a funny/not funny story. I'm standing up on the train getting ready to get off in Newark. Now, the bars/handrails on those trains (or any NYC subway) are just infected with pure nastiness. So I'm barely holding on with two fingers on this crowded train when it suddenly jerks and my whole hand slips forward, punching a woman square in the face. She dropped her phone and cracked the screen. I swear this shit can only happen to me!

She was not happy, and clearly hurt but I apologized profusely, it was a total accident. I felt horrible, but it was still funny. I think if I was a witness instead of the culprit, I'd bust out laughing!

Diary Entry - Sometime in 1993

This was a time where I was just starting to think about what I wanted to do with the rest of my life and I was pretty much fed up with the day job I had in Eatontown, New Jersey, where I worked for five, painstakingly long years. I had a boss that no matter what, she would always find some way to fuck up my mood and my day. Part of my job responsibilities as an accounting clerk, I had to make daily bank deposits at two different banks. I would also make the coffee for the morning and afternoon breaks and buy the milk, cream and miscellaneous supplies for the break room. In exchange for all of this, I would receive two-and-a-half additional hours of pay per week and $10.00 cash for gas in my car. My boss would use my daily bank runs as an excuse for me to do her errands as well (pick up prescriptions, drop off or pick up dry cleaning, pick up her lunch, etc.).

One morning I was feeling generous and I decided to pick up a cup of coffee from the local convenience store for everyone in my department (there were only four of us) - biggest mistake ever!! That became a morning ritual. I had to run out every fucking morning to get this prissy, bitch of a boss, her hazelnut coffee with milk. She wasn't the most pleasant person to deal with on a daily basis and she often poked fun at my expense, which was almost a daily occurrence.

One day she had belittled me so much, then suddenly decided to be nice to me because she needed her coffee. Mind you, I didn't care because I used it as an excuse to get out of the office for a bit, and I also picked up coffee for myself and my other two colleagues, and it was much better than what we were serving in the break room!

So, I went to the store, got her coffee just the way she wanted it. But, I was so annoyed and seething because I was so fed up with her bullshit, snarky comments and treating me like her personal slave, that I sat in my car for a few minutes and began to ponder the thought of leaving that stupid job and finding something better for myself. Her big face kept appearing in my thoughts and it angered me. I opened up her coffee cup, took a giant swig, swished that shit around in my mouth and spit it back in her cup, then hocked a loogie on top of that, all while mumbling to myself, "Take that, Count Bitchula!"

On my way back to the office, I had to park in the far end of the parking lot in the pouring rain and walk with the tray of coffee without an umbrella back to the office building. Now I'm drenched, my clothes are a wrinkled mess, my hair was flat (at a time where big hair was still "in", sorta) and my mascara ran down my cheeks like tiny, black veins.

But I got that bitch her coffee!!

I set my cup of coffee and purse on my desk, handed out the other cups to my boss and co-workers, making sure I handed my boss the right cup, then headed toward the break room to make the coffee for the morning break. My colleague, who sat across the desk from me, followed me into the break room to gossip. She began to tell me how they were making fun of me after I left for the bank. I was steaming, again, and while I should have kept this information to myself, I blurted out to my co-worker that I had spit in her coffee. She appeared shocked at first but then burst out laughing.

"Oh my god, you did not!" She said, as her face turned beet red with laughter.

"Oh yes I did! And that bitch deserves it!" I said, as we both headed back toward our office. She was still red in the face but was composing her laughter as we both sat down at our desks.

My boss sipped her coffee as I looked across the room at her.

"Mmm, this coffee is so good. Thank you!" She said, with a look on her face like she just had the most intense orgasm.

"Oh, you are most welcome!" I smiled, as she took another sip and swallowed.

I caught sight of my co-worker across the desk from me and to this day, I am not sure how I kept my composure. She was nearly purple, silently laughing as the tears rolled down her cheeks as she knew what I had just done. She suddenly got up and left the room, wiping away the tears.

My boss looked at me and said with annoyed sarcasm, "What's *her* problem?" I shrugged my shoulders and walked out behind her as it was now our break time. I walked outside to find my co-worker smoking a cigarette and laughing hysterically.

So what's the moral of *this* story you ask? It's quite simple really. Never piss me off then ask me to pick up your coffee!

Diary Entry - Sometime in 1994

I was just starting to plan my wedding and my fiancé was still in college up in Boston. I was feeling rather lonely and needed some time out with friends. I decided to plan a night out at a local bar in Red Bank. For those who don't know Monmouth County New Jersey, Red Bank is a hip and quaint, little town where the nightlife is much like a mini New York City, minus the lines to get into the trendy clubs.

I picked up a friend and met some other friends out at bar. We were all talking and dancing and having a good time when an acquaintance suggested that her and I go to up to the bar and do a shot (aww shit, this can't be good!) She orders us shots of Jagermeister, which was a liquor that I hadn't heard of at that time (I was barely over the legal drinking age, what the hell did I know about liquor?!) Feeling in such a good mood as I was, I said "sure, why not!"

The bartender handed us the shots. I was about to do the shot when she hands me a straw. "Here, you get buzzed faster if you drink the shot through a straw." I agreed, we toasted, then sipped the shot quickly through the straw.

Let's fast forward a bit to where I'm now at the bar for shot number four of this Jagermeister that I suddenly loved for that short while. Shot number four, coupled with two drinks of Sex on the

Beach, and a beer, I was now drunk. A guy friend we were with noticed that I was drunk and suggested to my friend that she take me home. I wasn't ready to leave yet but I was so glad that I did. She held onto me as she walked me to my car. She fumbled through my tiny purse for my car keys and put me in the passenger seat. She got in the car and started the 15 minute drive back to her apartment.

During those 15 minutes, I rolled down the window and began to puke as the rain hit me in the face. I laid my head out of the window and rested it on the door and allowed the cold air and rain to hit my face. It felt good on my skin. At some point I passed out with my head out the window.

We arrived at my friend's apartment and she was trying to wake me up to get me out of the car. I drove a pretty hot sports car back then with low bucket seats. She leaned across me to open the passenger door. Still trying to wake me up, she decided that she needed to get me out of the car so she swung her legs over the center console and pushed me out of the car with her feet. I fell out of the car, face down in a puddle of mud.

At this point she ran around to my side of the car to get me up and out of the mud. Her neighbor, who lived downstairs, pulled up behind us. He saw her struggling to get me on my feet and decided to help.

I'm covered in mud and puke, but they somehow managed to get me up on my feet and swung my arms over each of their shoulders. My friend cracked a joke to her neighbor as I was barely conscious at this point. I remember looking at him, then puking on him! Poor guy! They got me inside and laid me face down on the floor of her living room. Still clothed in my jacket and boots and my long, puke and mud-drenched hair sprawled out around me. They left me there for the night.

Somewhere around 8:00 am, I woke up quickly. I knew I had to get home and I was dizzy and nauseous, but I grabbed my purse and keys and left. I got into my car and saw the dried puke that had somehow come back in the window and ended up splattered against my entire back seat. I groaned as I realized that I would need to clean that up as quickly as possible. The smell in my car was unbearable. Aside from the puke, I couldn't quite put my finger on the odor that lingered. I knew I had dried mud in my hair and I reeked of stale perfume, cigarette smoke and puke, but there was something else. As I drove, I checked my shoes to make sure that I didn't accidentally step in dog shit during my drunken shenanigans the night before. Nope, all clear.

I kept going over and over in my mind what I was going to tell my mother when I got home. I hadn't told her that I wasn't coming home, and rightfully so! I was a hot, fucking mess, literally! But there would be no hiding it from her. The evidence was all over the side of my car and in the back seat and I was covered in dried puke and mud from head to toe. I was doomed.

I pulled into my driveway and said about a dozen "Hail Mary's" that my mother wasn't going to freak out on me. I was 22 years old, a "legally" responsible adult, yet I was still petrified of my mother. I'm sure she was worried sick because I never once ever gave her a reason to worry about me when I went out because I always came home......until that night.

To my surprise, my mother's car was not in the driveway, however my mom and my aunt were holding a garage sale that day and my mother would have moved the car because it blocked prime real estate for displaying the items for sale. But, she wasn't even parked in the street. She wasn't home! I thought to myself, *"Perfect, I have time to hop in the shower quickly before she gets home."*

I walked into my house to hear the vacuum cleaner running and my aunt was frantically pushing it around the dining room. She looked up at me and said "Oh, hello….." as I quickly watched the smile on her face turn to one of disgust and disappointment. She followed up by saying, "You look like shit! What happened to you? Your mother is worried sick!" I just held up my hand in a very *'talk to the hand, girlfriend'* manner and didn't say a word, walked down the hall to my bedroom where I took off my boots, jacket and threw my purse on the bed.

(And this is where it gets good, folks!)

I took my bathrobe and headed for the bathroom to shower. With a hangover from hell, I could not wait to wash it all away with shampoo and body wash. I began to undress, first taking off my sweater and bra, then my socks. I unbuttoned my jeans and pulled them down, along with them came my underwear and what appeared to be a giant, squished Hershey's Kiss!

I was overwhelmed by the stench and realized that it was the same smell I had been smelling in the car ride home! I shit my fucking pants and I had no idea! How the hell did that happen?? I had no recollection of the night before other than puking my guts out. I can only assume that I "had one on the chamber" already and the extreme force of my stomach muscles not only emptied the contents of my stomach, but also my colon! (I know now that this is true because many years later I came down with the flu and needed to have a bucket in my lap while I sat on the toilet!)

I lingered for a bit and let the water wash over me, hoping for a miracle that would somehow make the nausea subside. I finished up and went back to my room where I collapsed on my bed and went to sleep. The confrontation with my mother, well, I will just leave that to your imagination! For those that know me and my mom, know how it all went down!

A few days later I'm on the phone with my friend who drove me home that night. To add insult to injury on a night that I just wanted to forget – and never drink Jagermeister again – she proceeded to tell me that, other than what I've just told all of you, her brother and his friend came over to her apartment to hang out at 2:00 a.m. since the bars were closed and they weren't quite ready to finish up their night of debauchery and drunken shenanigans just yet.

They all sat there, laughed and poked fun at me and admitted that they have all had nights like mine (a drunk, puking, mud-soaked, embarrassing mess!) I never even heard them come in or anything that happened after I passed out, face down on her living room floor, with my ass in the air and a giant, squished Hershey's Kiss wedged ever so snugly in my butt! I'm sure I must have smelled pretty foul!

Now while this story would be killed, burned or buried without witness for most people, whether you want to admit it or not, this is the type of shit that happens to the best of us all at one time or another during our lives. And while most would rather forget these embarrassing tales, they are funny to tell years down the road. If you can find humor in these embarrassing moments, it will keep you human and humble.

But all I have to say about this particular event is.....thank God that camera phones were not yet in existence yet, and the internet was still in the developing stages or my ass would have been all over YouTube! Ugh!

So, in conclusion kids......

There is always stuff happening around us.
Some of it is just so damn funny and some of it is
just too off-the-wall to be believed. But either way,
we just need to stop and take a look once in a while
and you will find it.

And there you have it. While this book idea
took many years, plus a few months to write, I
finally did it! I know that there are many stories
that I have missed but perhaps that should be saved
for Volume II of this ongoing diary.

<u>*Special Thanks*</u>

My husband Marc, my daughter Emily and my extended family and close friends for their love, support and encouragement through this entire process.

My loving and encouraging friends who are always there for me, pushing me forward, and whom I hold dear to my heart, My BFF Laura B., Ana V., Lisa C., Linda H., Kristy K., Ruth C. & Ali V.

My extended Kohl's 0693 family – Yorki, Allison, Angela, Nancy, Rena, Aida, Andrea, John, MargaretAnn, Linda, Maryann, Kristy, Bob, Ryan, Carolyn, Madeline, Susan, Rhonda, Patricia & Patrick (and anyone else I may have missed by name!) for putting up with my silly shenanigans!

Lisa Cohen for her support, encouragement and editing! You rock!

Cindy Anderson for her patience and brilliant illustration and layout design for the cover.

John Ahrens for his support and great photos for the book!

My friend, and fellow author, D. Allen for his inspiration and character design for the cover. Without his partnership on our book, **Bedtime Stories: His Words, Her Desires**, *I would not have continued to pursue my lifelong dream as a writer.*

Fran H., Lisa A., Jackie A., Holly G. & Stephanie J. for helping D. Allen and I get the word out on **Bedtime Stories**. *Whether you know it or not, you have all played a key role in my decision to keep moving forward despite all obstacles. For that, I am forever grateful!*

All of the various commuters, tourists and native New Yorkers, for without your quirkiness, antics and attitude, none of these stories would have been possible!

Finally, I would like to thank all of my readers and followers on all social media platforms. I am forever humbled for your continued support as it's what has kept me motivated and I look forward to many more writings for your enjoyment.

Sandy C. Jayne

Made in the USA
Middletown, DE
05 May 2022